# PRAISE FOR JENNIFER CHANDLER AND
## *THE SOUTHERN PANTRY COOKBOOK*

Jennifer Chandler's *The Southern Pantry Cookbook* is every new, or inexperienced, cook's best friend. From stocking a pantry, to selecting the right kitchen tools, the information is presented in a sharp, crisp, and understandable manner that is all Jennifer. What I l really admire are the quick and easy recipes that will lead readers, along with their family and guests, to enjoy delightful recipes for years to come. I give it a big Yum's Up!

MARK H. KELLY, LODGE MANUFACTURING COMPANY. CONTRIBUTOR TO *THE LODGE CAST IRON COOKBOOK* AND *LODGE CAST IRON NATION COOKBOOK*

Jennifer Chandler is an incredibly talented recipe writer, and her clever new *The Southern Pantry Cookbook* empowers people—wherever they live—to make scrumptious Southern food TONIGHT!

MATT LEE AND TED LEE, AUTHORS OF *THE LEE BROS. CHARLESTON KITCHEN*

I love this book! Jennifer Chandler wants to get everybody cooking, and her latest book shows exactly how to do so with pleasure and success. She shares smart tips for setting up your pantry, fridge, and freezer shelves, and offers more than 100 clear, can-do Southern recipes for speedy suppers, luscious picnics, and memorable Sunday dinners. Gorgeous photos showcase both classic dishes and inspired fare. Jambalaya Pasta; Cheddar-Pecan Shortbread; Sweet Corn Pudding; Old-Fashioned Caramel Pie. . . . the only problem for me is what to make first?

NANCIE MCDERMOTT, AUTHOR OF *SOUTHERN CAKES: SWEET AND IRRESISTIBLE RECIPES FOR EVERYDAY CELEBRATIONS*

I've cleaned out my pantry, re-evaluated my freezer space, heck, I've actually looked differently at Southern cooking since taking a look at Jennifer Chandler's new book, *The Southern Pantry Cookbook: 105 Recipes Already Hiding in Your Kitchen*. What a great guide to simplifying the art of Southern cooking. And my, oh, my, those Fried Pork Medallions with Milk Gravy, just awesome!

FRED THOMPSON, AUTHOR OF *SOUTHERN SIDES: 250 DISHES THAT REALLY MAKE THE PLATE* AND NINE OTHER COOKBOOKS; PUBLISHER OF *EDIBLE PIEDMONT*

In a time when it feels we all are running in opposite directions, Jennifer shows you that you can put a delicious supper on the table without another trip to the grocery store.

STACEY LITTLE, AUTHOR OF *THE SOUTHERN BITE*

Jennifer has been a guest in my kitchen at my restaurant, a guest in my home on the bookshelf, and now with *The Southern Pantry* will have another seat at my table. These time-tested and quick recipes are great for any home cook, from a novice to a well-seasoned one.

KELLY ENGLISH, *FOOD & WINE* BEST NEW CHEF 2009; CHEF/OWNER, THE ACCLAIMED RESTAURANT IRIS AND THE SECOND LINE

In this book, Jennifer shows us that Southern food is about so much more than just ribs and BBQ. The home-cooked meals in this book are rich in flavor and tradition.

NICK VERGOS, CHEF/CO-OWNER, THE AWARD-WINNING CHARLIE VERGOS' RENDEZVOUS

Imagine the soul of your favorite family recipes updated and curated by an accomplished chef who understands how to help you put an amazing meal on the table in a flash--that's the beauty of *The Southern Pantry Cookbook*. Jennifer Chandler makes crafting stylish Southern family meals simple, satisfying, and always delicious.

JUSTIN FOX BURKS AND AMY LAWRENCE, AUTHORS OF *THE SOUTHERN VEGETARIAN: 100 DOWN-HOME RECIPES FOR THE MODERN TABLE*

Jennifer's Southern cooking is so good even a Master Chef is interested in the recipes in her book *The Southern Pantry Cookbook*!

JOSÉ GUTIERREZ, MAÎTRE CUISINIER DE FRANCE MASTER CHEF OF THE YEAR 2011; CHEF/OWNER, RIVER OAKS

For the beginning cook, *The Southern Pantry Cookbook* is a perfect roadmap for stocking up and cooking out of a home kitchen. For those of us who have cooked with Jennifer's books before, this is another batch of scrumptious, bullet-proof, company-worthy recipes to add to the rotation.

MELISSA PETERSEN, EDITOR AND PUBLISHER, *EDIBLE MEMPHIS* MAGAZINE

It's fitting that chef Jennifer Chandler's first few books all start with the word "Simply." Her food is simply delicious, and *The Southern Pantry Cookbook* continues that trend–the recipes all look like they'd be fun to try, and a lot more fun to eat.

ANDY MEEK, JOURNALIST

Jennifer Chandler once again combines her love and knowledge of fine cooking with the practical experience of a working mom. Her recipes are easy to follow, easy to adapt (she even gives suggestions), and best of all, delicious. In her fourth book, Jennifer delivers our traditional Southern favorites with practical advice on stocking a kitchen that beginners will find indispensable and with tips that will make even seasoned cooks say "Aha!" Whether cooking for your family or entertaining friends, *The Southern Pantry Cookbook* is one you'll pull out again and again.

JENNIFER BIGGS, FOOD WRITER, *THE COMMERCIAL APPEAL*

If Memphis had a goodwill ambassador of family cooking, Jennifer Chandler would wear the crown. Southern by birth but healthy by inclination, Chandler's recipes in *The Southern Pantry Cookbook* reflect her talent and charm: They are personable, delicious, and destined to become longtime friends.

Pamela Denney, food editor of Memphis magazine

Her love for cooking is "simply" contagious and she makes the kitchen an inviting place for even the most novice of cooks. Jennifer's cookbooks introduce us to delicious recipes that are enjoyable to cook, easy on the taste buds, and leave us feeling like a champ in the kitchen. It doesn't get much better than that!

Lauren Patterson, Style Blueprint

Jennifer fills this book with her characteristic joy and sense of fun in the kitchen. *The Southern Pantry Cookbook* showcases her ingenuity and is a close second to having her actually with you in the kitchen.

Andy Ticer and Michael Hudman, Food & Wine Best New Chefs 2013; chefs/<br>owners of the acclaimed Andrew Michael Italian Kitchen and Hog and Hominy;<br>authors of Collards & Carbonara: Southern Cooking, Italian Roots

# THE Southern Pantry COOKBOOK

## 105 RECIPES ALREADY HIDING IN YOUR KITCHEN

**JENNIFER CHANDLER**

*Enjoy!*

*Jennifer Chandler*

NELSON
BOOKS

An Imprint of Thomas Nelson

Published in Nashville, Tennessee, by Nelson Books, an imprint of Thomas Nelson. Nelson Books and Thomas Nelson are registered trademarks of HarperCollins Christian Publishing, Inc.

Design by Walter Petrie

Photography by Justin Fox Burks

Thomas Nelson, Inc., titles may be purchased in bulk for educational, business, fund-raising, or sales promotional use. For information, please e-mail SpecialMarkets@ThomasNelson.com.

**Library of Congress Cataloging-in-Publication Data**

Chandler, Jennifer, 1970-
  The southern pantry cookbook : 105 recipes already hiding in your kitchen / Jennifer Chandler.
    pages cm
  ISBN 978-1-4016-0521-6 (hardback)
  1. Cooking, American—Southern style. I. Title.
  TX715.2.S68C44 2014
  641.5975—dc23                                                                        2014007739

*Printed in the United States of America*

14 15 16 17 18 QG 6 5 4 3 2 1

As with everything I do with love,
this book is dedicated to Paul, Hannah, and Sarah.

# CONTENTS

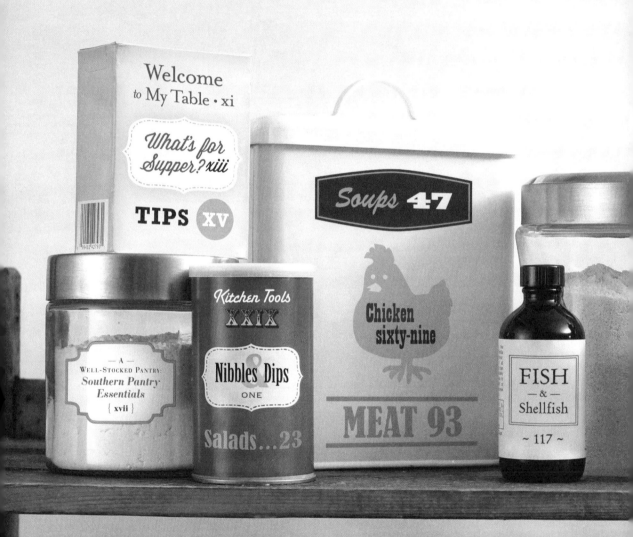

# WELCOME TO MY TABLE

I AM A SOUTHERN GIRL THROUGH AND THROUGH. ALL I HAVE TO DO IS open my mouth and my drawl gives it away. Born in Louisiana and raised in Tennessee, I feel blessed to have enjoyed the best of what the South has to offer.

My dad's family is from New Orleans, and in my opinion, his mom was the best cook in the world. This demure French Creole woman could cook up a storm. I don't think I ever had a meal from her kitchen that was not delicious. She made everything from scratch and always used the best ingredients she could find. Even her simple ham and cheese po' boys were divine. And how she could make perfect divinity and meringues on the most humid of New Orleans days, I sadly will never know. I have vivid memories of standing on my tiptoes to peer into the pot of gril-lades simmering on her stove top. It's a dish that she served with love at family gatherings, and following in her footsteps, I do the same for my family now.

My mother's parents were from Alabama, and the dishes Grandma Boone served us were totally different from my other grandmother's Louisiana fare, but equally delicious. Grandma Boone could fry up the crispiest catfish with just a simple cornmeal batter. Her cakes had no rivals.

The dishes of my South range from spicy Louisiana fare to down-home country cooking. My table has been a melting pot of the best foods of the South. The spices and a few ingredients may differ, but the common denominator is that these dishes were cooked with a loving hand. Now you see why I said I have been blessed!

So much of Southern living is spent in the kitchen and around the dinner table. My most cherished memories of my family are centered around a meal. The recipes I share with you in this book are family traditions., recipes that remind us of how a meal can bring the comfort of good food and good company. No fancy restaurant in the world can offer food as good as what is made in a Southern kitchen with love.

The good news about Southern home-cooking is that if you have a well-stocked pantry, you can easily whip up a delicious meal without having to rush to the store. In *The Southern Pantry Cookbook*, I show you how to prepare delicious Southern dishes using the household staples you already have in your kitchen. The recipes in this book are easy, no-fuss Southern favorites. Some are very traditional. Others have a tasty spin on a classic recipe. But they all boil down to making good food that is simply delicious.

I have made sure to include useful information on ingredients, techniques, storage, shortcuts, variations, and substitutions that will help you make cooking dinner a breeze. Cooking supper should be fun . . . not feel like a chore.

I have also included a guideline of what a well-stocked Southern pantry should look like. One of the many beauties of Southern cooking is that all the ingredients are simple and can be found at your neighborhood grocery store. If you have the ingredients on my list, you will have enough food on hand to prepare a delicious and satisfying meal at a moment's notice.

My hope is that you and your family enjoy these recipes . . . and many memorable meals together.

Happy cooking, y'all!

# WHAT'S FOR SUPPER?

IT'S A DAILY QUESTION. WHETHER EATING ALONE OR FEEDING OTHERS, you will ask yourself (or be asked): "What's for supper?"

It is simple to pull together delicious home-cooked meals if you are equipped with a few strategies.

- Maintain a well-stocked kitchen (see page xiii for my Well-Stocked Pantry list). Having the right ingredients in your pantry, refrigerator, and freezer can make the difference between ordering take-out pizza and having a delicious last-minute meal.
- Arm yourself with a repertoire of basic cooking techniques. When choosing the recipes to share in this book, I intentionally included a variety of cooking skills. Sautéing, pan roasting, braising, baking, and sauce making are all simple techniques that can be used to make an infinite number of dishes.
- Make it easy on yourself and take the stress out of cooking. Use shortcut ingredients like rotisserie chickens. Frozen vegetables are also a great short-cut since they are picked and frozen at the peak of ripeness to lock in flavor and nutrients.
- Do whatever you can in advance, keeping in mind that some dishes actually taste better the next day. Make double batches of recipes that freeze well so you will always have a home-cooked meal available in the freezer.

- Use the best ingredients. The key to delicious food is simple: use fresh, in-season, top-quality ingredients. And remember, best does not always mean the most expensive. Let flavor be your guide when choosing what goes into your food.
- Taste as you go. By tasting a spoonful here and there throughout the cooking process, you will see if you need to add a little more of something. And always be sure to taste your dish before serving to make sure you don't need one more dash of salt or pepper or a tablespoon of cream or butter to round out the flavor.

# TIPS

WHAT ARE THE QUESTIONS YOU OFTEN HAVE WHEN READING A RECIPE?
"What can I do ahead?" "Can I freeze this?" "What is a good substitute?"

I tried to think of all the different tips and variations that I wished the cookbooks on my shelves offered. Here are six basic tips you will find throughout this book that will help you get delicious meals on the table . . . even on your busiest day.

**COOKING TIPS:** Detailed information about cooking techniques and specific ingredients.

**PANTRY SHORTCUTS:** Substitutes and shortcuts to save a little time in the kitchen.

**VARIATIONS:** Tips on how to put a unique spin on a classic dish.

**DO-AHEAD:** Tips and strategies to take the stress out of dinnertime.

**FREEZES WELL:** Dishes that are perfect for freezing.

**WEEKNIGHT CLASSICS:** Dishes that can easily be whipped up in about 30 minutes or less.

# A WELL-STOCKED PANTRY

*Southern Pantry Essentials*

WHEN PREPARING MEALS, IT IS IMPORTANT TO HAVE A WELL-STOCKED pantry. If you're not sure what your pantry should look like, follow my essential pantry ingredients list on the next few pages. That way, when the time comes, you can prepare a delicious meal without having to run to the store.

## PASTA AND GRAINS

**Dried pastas (in all your favorite sizes and shapes):** *for eating plain or with a sauce*

**Grits (instant and stone-ground):** *for a side or casserole topping*

**Quinoa:** *great for using in soups, casseroles, or as a side dish*

**Rice (white and wild):** *great for using in soups, salads, casseroles, or as a side dish*

Store grains and rice in glass jars to keep them fresh.

I prefer long-grain rice to medium- or short-grain rice because it is fluffier and stays more separate when cooked.

## ON THE SHELF

**Bread crumbs (panko and plain):** *for topping casseroles or adding as a filler*

**Canned tomatoes (whole, diced, crushed, and paste):** *for sauces, soups, stews, and casseroles*

**Chicken stock:** *for the base of soups and sauces as well as the ideal liquid for braising meats*

**Cornbread mix:** *a great shortcut as well as base for many sides*

**Dried and canned beans (black-eyed peas, black, navy, kidney, garbanzo):** *for soups, stews, and a multitude of main and side dishes*

**Dried cranberries:** *to throw in salads or baked goods for flavor and texture, as well as great for snacking*

**Jarred marinara sauce:** *a great shortcut ingredient for pastas, casseroles, and pizzas*

**Canned diced green chilies:** *for giving soups, casseroles, and dips a Tex-Mex flair*

**Diced pimientos or roasted red peppers:** *for salads and dips*

**Nuts (pecans, walnuts, peanuts):** *to throw in salads or baked goods for flavor and texture; to use as a crunchy topping; also great for snacking*

**Olives (green and Kalamata):** *for snacking as well as adding to savory dishes*

**Jarred marinated artichokes:** *an easy add-in for salads, pastas, and dips*

Unlike most canned vegetables, canned tomatoes offer flavor just as intense as ripe tomatoes.

## BAKING INGREDIENTS

**All-purpose flour:** *for baking and thickening sauces*
**Baking powder:** *a leavening agent for baking*
**Baking soda:** *a leavening agent for baking*
**Chocolate chips:** *for cookies, bars, melting, and snacking*
**Sugar (white, light brown, and powdered):** *for adding sweetness to just about anything*
**Pure vanilla extract:** *the essential flavoring for baked goods*
**Unsweetened cocoa:** *for baking chocolate goodies*
**Yellow cornmeal:** *for cornbread, batters, and adding texture to dishes*

To keep it fresher and to keep bugs out, I store my flour and cornmeal in the freezer in freezer-safe resealable bags.

To keep brown sugar soft, I put it in a resealable plastic bag, squeeze out all excess air, seal, and then store in an airtight container.

To soften hardened brown sugar, add a moist paper towel to the plastic storage bag and microwave for 20 to 30 seconds.

## CONDIMENTS

**Assorted jams and jellies:** *for spreading on breads as well as making dressings and sauces*

**Assorted vinegars (red wine, cider, white wine, and balsamic):** *for making dressings and adding acidity to dishes*

**Barbecue sauce:** *for basting meats*

**Honey:** *the all-natural sweetener, good for sweetening dishes as well as drizzling over biscuits*

**Hot sauce:** *for adding a spicy kick to a dish; choose based on flavor not heat*

**Ketchup:** *to add flavor to dishes and a glaze for meatloaf*

**Maple syrup or molasses:** *for drizzling over pancakes, as well as adding a rich sweetness to dishes*

**Mustards (whole grain, Dijon, and yellow):** *the base for dressings and sauces*

**Olive oil:** *my go-to fat for cooking food; adds a nice fruity flavor*

**Salsa:** *a quick appetizer, plus it can be used in place of tomatoes in many dishes*

**Soy sauce:** *to add a salty richness to a dish*

**Vegetable or canola oil:** *neutral-flavored oils that are ideal for frying because of their high smoke point*

**Worcestershire sauce:** *to flavor meat dishes, as well as some Creole dishes, like barbecued shrimp*

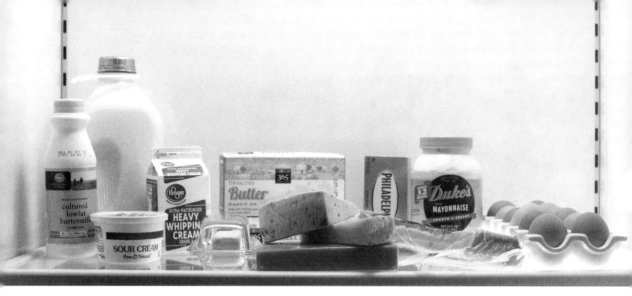

## IN THE REFRIGERATOR

**Bacon:** *this cured meat is not just for breakfast; use it to add flavor to dishes*

**Buttermilk:** *a key ingredient in Southern baking*

**Cheeses (Parmesan, Cheddar, shredded mozzarella, and blue):** *for adding to just about any dish—warm or cold*

**Cream cheese:** *for adding creaminess to dishes and desserts; makes a simple appetizer when pepper jelly is spooned over a block*

**Eggs:** *essential for just about everything*

**Mayonnaise:** *a condiment that also adds richness to dishes; it can also be used to help bind a crust to a meat*

**Milk:** *use 2% or whole milk for cooking; skim milk is too watery*

**Sour cream:** *a condiment that can be used to add a tangy richness to a dish*

**Unsalted butter:** *fresher in flavor and more versatile for cooking and baking than salted*

## FRESH PRODUCE

**Baby carrots:** *for snacking, a side, and an ingredient in numerous dishes*

**Bell peppers (red and green):** *a key ingredient in adding flavor to raw and cooked Southern dishes*

**Cherry tomatoes:** *for snacking or tossing in salads, relishes, and pasta dishes*

**Celery:** *for snacking and adding flavor to soups, stews, and sauces; adds crunch to salads*

**Fresh herbs (basil, cilantro, and parsley):** *use to add flavor and color*

**Garlic:** *my favorite way to add flavor to a dish; look for heads with tightly packed cloves*

**Lemons:** *sunny lemons perk up almost everything with their bright, acidic juice; don't forget to use the zest too*

**Onions (yellow and red):** *for adding a bite to cold dishes and a sweet oniony flavor to cooked dishes*

**Potatoes (sweet and red-skin):** *for sides, salads, and soups; the small red potatoes are the most versatile variety*

Green bell pepper, onion, and celery are considered the "Holy Trinity" of Creole cooking. This combination is used as the base of almost every savory Louisiana dish.

A bag of baby carrots is not just for snacking. I turn to these peeled carrots when I need sliced carrots in a dish.

To keep your "tears" at a minimum, store your onions in the refrigerator crisper drawer.

## IN THE FREEZER

**Bread:** *for sandwiches, fillers, and bread crumbs*

**Chicken (boneless breasts as well as other chicken parts):** *for numerous entrées, soups, and salads*

**Flaked, sweetened coconut:** *for desserts, salads, and toppings*

**Frozen dinner rolls:** *for a quick and easy side*

**Frozen fruits (peaches and berries):** *for baked goods and smoothies*

**Frozen vegetables (okra, peas, green beans, corn, and spinach):** *perfect stand-ins for fresh veggies*

**Ground beef:** *for burgers, meatloaf, casseroles, and tacos; 20 percent fat (80/20) is ideal for juicy results*

**Nuts (pecans, pine nuts, walnuts, and almonds):** *for snacking and adding a nutritious crunch to a dish*

**Pork chops:** *for quick-fix suppers*

**Sausage (breakfast, Italian, and Andouille):** *for breakfast, appetizers, and main courses*

**Shrimp:** *keep both shell-on and peeled and deveined shrimp in your freezer for quick meals; they thaw in minutes in a colander under running cold water*

**Tortillas (corn and flour):** *for quesadillas, tacos, burritos, and adding texture to a dish*

**Unbaked piecrust:** *I prefer the ones in a box so I can roll the dough out and use for a multitude of sweet and savory dishes*

**Homemade sauces:** *keep containers of homemade tomato and meat sauces in your freezer for shortcut meals*

Meats are best thawed in the refrigerator. Keep in mind that large quantities could take a day or two to thaw.

Freeze meats and cooked dishes in small quantities for easy thawing.

Make sure all cooked dishes are chilled before freezing.

Frozen fruits are the perfect stand-ins for pies, crisps, and cobblers when the fresh fruits aren't in season.

## IN THE SPICE CABINET

**Black peppercorns for your peppermill:** *freshly ground pepper tastes far better than ground*

**Blackened seasoning:** *for adding a fiery Cajun kick to meat, chicken, or fish*

**Creole seasoning:** *for adding a taste of Louisiana to myriad dishes*

**Crushed red pepper flakes:** *for adding heat to a dish*

**Dried herbs (thyme, oregano, and basil):** *for adding flavor*

**Dried spices (cumin, cinnamon, chili powder, paprika):** *for adding flavor*

**Kosher salt:** *the essential ingredient to enhance the flavor of food*

Store spices and dried herbs in a cool, dark, and dry place. The heat from a stove top or oven as well as moisture can shorten their shelf life.

Buy small containers of spices you don't use that often.

Use a marker to label each spice with the date you open it.

Most spices last for one year if stored properly. Let taste and smell be your guidelines for whether or not they have lost their flavor.

Salt 101: I recommend kosher salt for cooking. Table salt has additives that affect how it flavors food in the cooking process. Whereas sea salt is a pure product, like kosher salt, it is not worth the extra expense, in my opinion.

I like to keep an herb garden in my kitchen so I always have fresh herbs available. Basil, thyme, rosemary, and flat-leaf parsley will all grow well on a sunny kitchen windowsill.

## A SEASONAL PANTRY

I always keep my pantry stocked with fresh, seasonal produce.

Seasonal produce not only tastes better but is less expensive. A strawberry grown down the street is fresher and will cost less than one picked a week before and shipped from across the country.

Most grocery stores now feature locally grown seasonal fruits and vegetables in their produce departments. Seasonal produce can also be found at your local farmers' markets, or you can grow them in your backyard garden or in potted plants.

Freeze seasonal veggies you grew in your garden or picked up at the market for that fresh-from-the-farm flavor year-round. Just blanch, dry, and freeze in your ideal portion sizes. Berries just need to be dried well and frozen, no need to blanch.

Freeze produce in the serving size you most often use.

For fruits like watermelon, apples, pears, and peaches, peel off the skins and dice or slice like you plan to use them before freezing. There is no need to blanch these fruits before freezing.

A vacuum sealer will help keep your frozen produce fresh longer.

Peel tomatoes before freezing. Use frozen tomatoes in soups and stews just like you would canned tomatoes.

## Spring Produce

Blackberries

Blueberries

Snow peas

Strawberries

## Summer Produce

Corn

Eggplant

Field peas

Okra

Peaches

Red and green bell peppers

Tomatoes (beefsteak, cherry, and green)

Watermelon

Yellow squash

Zucchini

## Fall Produce

Apples

Leafy greens (kale, Swiss chard, and collards)

Pears

Squash (butternut or acorn)

Sweet potatoes

# KITCHEN TOOLS

IF YOU HAVE THIS BASIC LIST OF KITCHEN UTENSILS ON HAND, MAKING THE recipes in this book will be effortless.

## Basic Kitchen Utensils

Set of graduated, straight-edge
    measuring cups made for dry
    ingredients
10-inch cast-iron skillet, well
    seasoned
Set of measuring spoons
12-inch ovenproof sauté pan
Glass liquid measuring cup
8-quart stockpot
Small whisk
2-quart saucepan with a lid
Tongs
Baking dishes (one 8 x 8-inch
    and one 9 x 13-inch)
Flat metal spatula
9-inch pie pan
Heatproof rubber spatula

Large rimmed baking sheet (also known as a jelly-roll pan)

Vegetable peeler (the rubber-handled ones are easier on your hands)

Colander

Can opener

Traditional four-sided cheese grater

Peppermill

Blender or food processor

Mixing bowls (both large and small)

Aluminum foil and plastic wrap

Good, sharp knives (a small paring knife and a 6- to 8-inch chef knife are a must)

Resealable containers and baggies (several sizes for leftovers)

Cutting boards (at least two: one for raw meats and another for everything else)

## Not Essential but Fun to Have

Garlic press

Fine sieve

Metal fish spatula

Removable-bottom tart pans

Microplane zesters (both fine and coarse)

7-quart Dutch oven (I love the enameled cast-iron ones)

Soup ladle

Stand mixer

Lemon juicer

Immersion blender

Organize your kitchen cabinets by the job. If you put everything back in its proper place, you should be able to find it blindfolded!

To prevent your cast-iron skillet from rusting, never wash it with soap! Instead, clean it with kosher salt, hot water, and paper towels. Always dry it completely before storing.

# NIBBLES AND DIPS

I LOVE TO HAVE GUESTS OVER FOR DINNER. SOME OF MY MOST FAVORITE memories have been sitting around the dinner table with good friends and family.

When having guests over, I want to offer them something to snack on while I am finishing up the meal. I set the appetizers up on my kitchen table so my guests can be in the kitchen with me while I am cooking. I want to spend time with them—not have them in another room while I'm in the kitchen!

Nibbles and dips that can be made in advance are my tried-and-true go-tos. Many of the items in this chapter, such as the Pickled Shrimp (page 11), Cheddar-Pecan Shortbread (page 4), and the Texas Caviar (page 20), can be made the day before. Items like the Tex-Mex Corn Dip (page 19) and Spicy Sausage Balls (page 15) can be assembled in the morning and then popped in the oven just before guests arrive.

Simple yet flavorful fare is my secret to easy entertaining.

# DEVILED EGGS

*Deviled eggs are the classic Southern party snack. They are a requisite for myriad events ranging from cocktail parties to summer picnic potlucks. What follows is a basic recipe, though there are many wonderful variations you can make.*

6 large eggs
1 tablespoon kosher salt, plus extra for
    seasoning
2 tablespoons mayonnaise
1 teaspoon Dijon mustard

1 teaspoon white wine vinegar
Dash of hot sauce
Freshly ground black pepper
Paprika, for garnish

Place the eggs in a medium saucepan and cover with cold water by 1 inch. Add 1 tablespoon of salt. Bring to a boil over high heat. As soon as it comes to a boil, remove the pan from the heat, cover, and let stand for 12 minutes. Place eggs in a colander to drain, and run cold water over them until cool.

Peel the eggs and cut in half lengthwise. Carefully remove the yolks, keeping the whites intact, and place the yolks in a medium bowl. Reserve the whites.

Using a fork, mash up the egg yolks. Add the mayonnaise, mustard, vinegar, and hot sauce, and stir until smooth. Season with salt and pepper to taste.

Spoon or pipe the egg yolk mixture into the whites. Cover with plastic wrap and refrigerate until ready to eat. Before serving, sprinkle with paprika.

**MAKES 12 DEVILED EGGS.**

**COOKING TIP:** *Adding a little salt to the cooking water and as peeling the eggs under cold water help make the peeling easier.*

## DEVILISHLY DELICIOUS DEVILED EGG ADD-INS

| | | |
|---|---|---|
| Smoked salmon and capers | Fresh herbs | Salsa |
| Crispy bacon | Curry powder | Horseradish |
| Sweet pickle relish | Chopped olives | Barbecue Dry Rub |

# CHEDDAR-PECAN SHORTBREAD

*Similar to cheese straws, these slice-and-bake savory cheese shortbreads are tasty nibbles for a cocktail party. I think they are the perfect complement to a glass of red wine.*

2 cups finely shredded sharp Cheddar
   cheese
1/2 cup (1 stick) unsalted butter,
   softened
1 cup all-purpose flour, plus extra for
   the work surface

1 teaspoon kosher salt
1/4 teaspoon cayenne pepper
2 cups finely chopped pecans
2 large egg whites, lightly beaten

Place the cheese, butter, flour, salt, and cayenne in the bowl of a food processor. Process until the dough just begins to form a ball, about 10 to 15 seconds.

Turn out the dough onto a floured work surface. Divide into two equal pieces. Roll each piece into a 1 1/2-inch thick log. Wrap each log with plastic wrap and refrigerate until firm, at least 2 hours or overnight.

Preheat the oven to 350 degrees. Line two baking sheets with parchment paper.

Place the pecans in a shallow bowl or baking dish. Unwrap the dough, and brush each log with the beaten egg whites. Roll the logs in the pecans to coat, pressing the pecans lightly to adhere. Slice each log crosswise into 1/4-inch rounds, and place on the prepared baking sheets at least 1 inch apart.

Bake until crisp, about 15 to 20 minutes. Let cool for 5 minutes on the baking sheets before transferring to a wire rack to cool completely.

**MAKES ABOUT 3 DOZEN.**

**Ⓥ VARIATION:** *Instead of having chopped pecans on the edges, you can also make the shortbread with 1 pecan half in the center of each cookie. To make this variation, prepare the dough as instructed. After chilling, slice each dough log, placing the slices onto the prepared baking sheets. Brush the slices with the egg whites and press a pecan into the center of each half. Bake as instructed above.*

**✓ DO-AHEAD:** *The Cheddar shortbread will keep for up to five days in an airtight container.*

# HOT ONION SOUFFLÉ DIP

*Oh my! This stuff is sinful. When I make it for a party, I have to hide it to make sure my family doesn't eat it before our guests arrive! I think it's best with corn chips, but you could use your favorite crackers or thinly sliced French bread as well.*

2 (8-ounce) packages cream cheese,
   softened
1/3 cup mayonnaise

1 1/3 cups grated Parmesan cheese
2 1/2 cups finely diced yellow onion
   (2 large onions)

Preheat the oven to 425 degrees.

In the bowl of an electric mixer, beat the cream cheese and mayonnaise until smooth. Add the Parmesan and onions, and stir until well combined.

Transfer the mixture to a 2-quart baking dish. Bake until golden brown and bubbly, 15 to 20 minutes. Serve warm.

**SERVES 8.**

**PANTRY SHORTCUT:** *Frozen onions can be substituted for fresh. Just be sure to thaw and press the onions with paper towels to remove the excess moisture before adding to the dip.*

**DO-AHEAD:** *This dip can be assembled up to one day in advance. Just allow 5 to 10 extra minutes' cooking time when heating straight from the refrigerator.*

# MEMPHIS SAUSAGE AND CHEESE PLATE

*A sausage and cheese plate is a tradition in Memphis barbecue shops. It's a quick and easy appetizer to put together for almost any affair.*

Vegetable oil, for the grates
1 link (14 ounces) smoked sausage
1/2 cup barbecue sauce, divided
4 tablespoons barbecue dry rub, divided

8 ounces Cheddar cheese, cut into sticks or cubes
Pickles, optional
Pepperoncini, optional

◻ Preheat a clean grill to medium-high with the lid closed for 8 to 10 minutes. Lightly brush the grates with oil.

◻ Evenly slather the sausage with 1/4 cup barbecue sauce. Season with 2 tablespoons of the dry rub.

◻ Place the sausage on the grill. Close the lid and cook, turning once, until browned and heated through, 3 to 4 minutes per side. Transfer the sausage to a cutting board and cut into 1/2-inch thick slices.

◻ To serve, arrange the sausage and cheese on a serving platter. Sprinkle the remaining 2 tablespoons of dry rub evenly over the top. Serve with the remaining 1/4 cup barbecue sauce on the side. Garnish with pickles and pepperoncini if desired.

**SERVES 6.**

🍳 **COOKING TIP:** *The sausage can be cooked indoors on a grill pan or in a cast-iron skillet.*

# PICKLED SHRIMP

*Classic shrimp cocktail gets a flavorful twist when the shrimp is pickled. It's so easy to make this elegant-looking party food with pantry staples. And as an added bonus, no cocktail dipping sauce is required since the marinade imparts so much flavor.*

3/4 cup white wine vinegar
1/4 cup freshly squeezed lemon juice
1/2 cup olive oil
1 tablespoon ground dry mustard
2 bay leaves
1 tablespoon whole black peppercorns
2 teaspoons kosher salt

3 pounds peeled and deveined large
    cooked shrimp (16/20 count), thawed
    if using frozen
1 cup thinly sliced yellow onion
    (1 large onion)
3 cloves garlic, minced
1 lemon, thinly sliced

In a large glass bowl stir together the vinegar, lemon juice, olive oil, dry mustard, bay leaves, peppercorns, and salt. Add the shrimp, onion, garlic, and lemon slices, and toss to coat. Cover and refrigerate for at least 8 hours or overnight. Remove the bay leaves and serve chilled.

**SERVES 12.**

**COOKING TIP:** *Be sure to marinate the shrimp in either a glass bowl or a resealable plastic bag. Avoid metal containers because they impart an unpleasant metallic taste to marinated foods.*

**DO-AHEAD:** *This dish actually tastes better when made the day before you plan to serve it. The extra time allows the flavors to all come together.*

# PIMENTO CHEESE

*There are not many foods as Southern as pimento cheese. I like to serve it at parties as a dip with pretzels and celery sticks.*

1 (3-ounce) package cream cheese, softened
1/2 cup mayonnaise
1/2 teaspoon sugar
3 cups shredded sharp Cheddar cheese

1 (4-ounce) jar finely diced pimentos, drained
Kosher salt
Freshly ground black pepper
Dash of hot sauce, optional

In a large bowl stir together the cream cheese, mayonnaise, and sugar until smooth. Add the cheese and the pimentos. Stir, mashing with a fork, until well combined and relatively smooth. Season with salt and pepper to taste. Add a dash of the hot sauce if desired. Cover and refrigerate until ready to use.

**SERVES 4 TO 6.**

**COOKING TIP:** *Roasted red peppers can be used in place of the pimentos. I prefer the texture of the pimento cheese when I shred the Cheddar cheese myself. But if you are in a hurry, you can use packaged shredded cheese.*

**DO-AHEAD:** *This recipe makes approximately 3 1/2 cups of pimento cheese. Pimento cheese will keep for up to four days in your refrigerator (if it lasts that long!).*

## 5 USES FOR PIMENTO CHEESE

A dip

A sandwich spread

A topping for burgers

A filling for bite-size tartlets

A cheesy omelet

## WEIGHTS AND MEASUREMENTS OF CHEESE

Most of you know that 8 ounces equals a cup, right? Well, guess what? That's not the case with cheese! Grated and shredded cheese is sold by weight, not volume. So when buying grated or shredded cheese, know that 4 ounces in weight equals 1 cup in volume.

# SPICY SAUSAGE BALLS

*In the South, sausage isn't just for breakfast. These spicy sausage balls are always a favorite on the buffet table for both elegant and casual events. Many of my friends serve it with a simple Dijonnaise dipping sauce. Just mix together 1/2 cup mayonnaise and 2 tablespoons Dijon mustard.*

1 cup all-purpose flour
1 1/4 teaspoons baking powder
Kosher salt and freshly ground pepper
2 cups finely shredded sharp Cheddar
   cheese

1 pound hot breakfast sausage
2 tablespoons unsalted butter, melted
   and cooled to room temperature

Preheat the oven to 400 degrees. Line 2 baking sheets with parchment paper.

In a large bowl whisk together the flour and baking powder. Season with salt and pepper to taste. Add the cheese, and toss to coat. Add the sausage and butter, and mix until well combined.

Roll the mixture into 1-inch balls. Place the balls, 1 inch apart, on the baking sheets. Bake until golden brown and cooked through, about 20 minutes.

**MAKES ABOUT 2 DOZEN.**

**COOKING TIP:** *You can mix the ingredients by hand, but it tends to be fairly sticky. Using a stand mixer with the dough hook attachment does the same trick with a lot less mess.*

**V** **VARIATION:** *For a not-so-spicy version, use mild breakfast sausage instead of the hot variety. Pepper Jack cheese would be a tasty substitute for the Cheddar.*

**FREEZES WELL:** *Freeze the sausage balls uncooked. If cooking from frozen, add about 5 more minutes to your cooking time.*

# CREAMY SPINACH DIP

*I love spinach dip! And to be honest, it's one of those dishes that truly tastes better when it's made with frozen spinach rather than fresh. I like to serve mine with salsa and sour cream on the side. A little of all three on a tortilla chip is a party in one bite!*

1 (10-ounce) package frozen chopped spinach, thawed and drained well
1 clove garlic, minced
1/2 cup grated Parmesan cheese
1 cup shredded mozzarella cheese, divided

1/2 cup sour cream
1/3 cup half-and-half
Dash of hot sauce
Kosher salt and freshly ground black pepper

▧ Preheat the oven to 350 degrees.

▧ In a medium bowl stir together the spinach, garlic, Parmesan, 3/4 cup of the mozzarella cheese, sour cream, half-and-half, and hot sauce until well combined. Season with salt and pepper to taste.

▧ Transfer the mixture to a 1-quart baking dish. Sprinkle the remaining 1/4 cup mozzarella evenly over the top.

▧ Bake until bubbly and the cheese is melted, 20 to 25 minutes. Serve warm.

**SERVES 6.**

🍴 **COOKING TIP:** *When using frozen spinach, it is very important to drain off all the excess water. I put my thawed spinach in a mesh strainer and press down on it to squeeze out as much water as possible.*

Ⓥ **VARIATION:** *If you have a jar of marinated artichoke hearts on hand, you can chop some up and add to the mixture before baking for a spinach-artichoke dip.*

✓ **DO-AHEAD:** *This dip can be assembled one day in advance. Store covered in the refrigerator until ready to bake.*

# TEX-MEX CORN DIP

*My friend Jenny Vergos is always whipping up something yummy. This simple dip is packed with flavor. Folks at your next party will be asking you for the recipe just like I asked Jenny.*

1 cup sour cream
1 cup mayonnaise
1 teaspoon garlic powder
3 cups corn kernels, thawed if using
   frozen
1 (4-ounce) jar diced pimentos, drained
1 (4-ounce) can chopped green chilies
3 cups shredded sharp Cheddar cheese
Kosher salt and freshly ground black
   pepper

▨ Preheat the oven to 350 degrees.

▨ In a large bowl stir together the sour cream, mayonnaise, and garlic powder. Add the corn, pimentos, green chilies, and cheese. Stir until well combined. Season with salt and pepper to taste.

▨ Place the mixture in a 2-quart baking dish. Bake until golden brown and bubbly, about 30 minutes. Serve warm.

**SERVES 6.**

**Ⓥ VARIATION:** *For a spicier dip, add ¼ cup diced jalapeños.*

**✅ DO-AHEAD:** *This dip can be assembled one day in advance. Store covered in the refrigerator until ready to bake.*

# TEXAS CAVIAR

*I am not sure how this dip got its name originally, but I'll take it over real caviar any day! This light and refreshing salsa is so versatile. Serve it as an appetizer with chips, as a side dish, or as a garnish for chicken or fish. Whichever way you choose, it is guaranteed to be a hit!*

2 (15-ounce) cans black-eyed peas,
    rinsed and drained
1/2 cup finely diced green bell pepper
    (1 small pepper)
1/2 cup finely diced red onion
    (1 small onion)
2 cloves garlic, minced

1/2 cup cherry tomatoes, quartered
1/4 cup red wine vinegar
2 tablespoons olive oil
1/2 teaspoon ground cumin
Kosher salt and freshly ground black
    pepper

In a medium bowl toss together the black-eyed peas, green pepper, onion, garlic, tomatoes, vinegar, olive oil, and cumin. Season with salt and pepper to taste. Cover and refrigerate until ready to serve. Serve chilled.

**SERVES 8.**

**COOKING TIP:** *For an extra zing, add a dash or two of your favorite hot sauce. Fresh cilantro would also be a nice addition.*

**DO-AHEAD:** *This dip can be made one day in advance. Cover and refrigerate until ready to serve.*

# SALADS

PANTRY STAPLES CAN MAKE THE MOST DELICIOUS SALADS. SOME OF THE salads in this chapter are best suited as the main course, whereas others are perfect sides.

The simplicity and versatility of most pantry staples allow you to be enormously creative when devising salad recipes. Salads are quick to prepare and impossible to mess up. You can make a salad with just about any food. It's as simple as tossing together a handful of flavorful ingredients. There really are no rules.

My first cookbook, *Simply Salads*, focused on salads made with leafy greens. The salads in this book are many of the composed salads that grace tables across the South. Traditional Southern dishes such as Southern Chicken Salad (page 37), Egg and Olive Salad (page 27), and Good Old Potato Salad (page 28) are perfect for your next luncheon or picnic. I also offer a modern spin on a few classic salads. I think you will love the fresh and bold flavors of my Roasted Sweet Potato Salad with Dried Cranberries and Pecans (page 41) and my Three-Bean Salad (page 42).

# CORN SALAD

*This simple salad is one of my summertime favorites. Light and refreshing, it is the perfect accompaniment to a piece of grilled chicken.*

4 cups corn kernels, thawed if using
    frozen
1 cup cherry tomatoes, quartered
1/2 cup finely diced red onion
    (1 small onion)
1/4 cup sour cream
2 tablespoons mayonnaise

2 tablespoons white wine vinegar
1/4 teaspoon ground dry mustard
Kosher salt and freshly ground black
    pepper
4 large basil leaves, sliced into thin
    strips

Bring a medium pot of salted water to a boil over high heat. Add the corn and cook until tender yet still crisp, about 5 minutes. Drain and cool to room temperature.

Place the corn, tomatoes, and onion in a large bowl.

In a small bowl whisk together the sour cream, mayonnaise, vinegar, and dry mustard until well combined. Pour the dressing over the corn mixture and toss to coat. Season with salt and pepper to taste. Gently stir in the basil. Cover and refrigerate until ready to serve. Serve chilled.

SERVES 6.

**COOKING TIP:** *A quick trick to cut basil into thin strips, also known as a chiffonade, is to place clean leaves in a pile, roll the leaves lengthwise, and thinly slice the roll crosswise.*

**DO-AHEAD:** *This salad can be made up to one day in advance. It is best to stir in the fresh basil just before serving.*

**WEEKNIGHT CLASSIC**

# EGG AND OLIVE SALAD

*Egg salad sandwiches are some of the easiest sandwiches in the world to make, especially if you have some hard-boiled eggs sitting around in the fridge. My family loves it with olives in the mix, but you can always omit the olives for a classic egg salad.*

6 hard-boiled large eggs, peeled and
    chopped (see page 2 for how to
    hard-boil eggs)
1 tablespoon Dijon mustard
2 tablespoons mayonnaise
1/4 teaspoon hot sauce

2 tablespoons minced yellow onion
2 tablespoons finely chopped green
    olives
Kosher salt and freshly ground black
    pepper

Place the chopped eggs in a medium bowl. Using a fork, mash up the eggs a little. Add the mustard, mayonnaise, hot sauce, onion, and olives. Stir to combine. Season with salt and pepper to taste. Serve chilled.

SERVES 4.

 **COOKING TIP:** *When mashing the eggs, don't overdo it. You want the egg mixture to have some texture. I like to "chop" my hard-boiled eggs by pushing them through the wire cooling rack I use for baking. I think this trick gives the salad the perfect texture.*

🎛 WEEKNIGHT CLASSIC

# GOOD OLD POTATO SALAD

*Potato salad comes in many guises, but I think this classic rendition may be my favorite. The whole grain mustard gives it a tangy bite.*

2 pounds small red potatoes, scrubbed
and cut into 1-inch pieces
1/4 cup finely diced red onion
(1/2 small onion)
1/2 cup thinly sliced celery (2 stalks)
1/4 cup mayonnaise

2 tablespoons sour cream
2 tablespoons whole grain mustard
1 teaspoon dried dill
Kosher salt and freshly ground black
pepper

Put the potatoes in a large pot and cover with cold water by 1 inch. Bring to a boil over high heat and then lower the temperature to a simmer. Cook just until they are tender but still firm, about 10 minutes. Drain and run under cold water to cool.

Place the drained potatoes, onions, and celery in a large bowl.

In a small bowl whisk together the mayonnaise, sour cream, mustard, and dill. Pour the dressing over the potato mixture and toss to coat. Season with salt and pepper to taste. Cover and refrigerate until ready to serve. Serve chilled.

SERVES 6.

>> **PANTRY SHORTCUT:** *To skip the step of cutting the potatoes, use frozen Southern-style hash brown potatoes in place of the red potatoes. Cook according to package directions.*

✓ **DO-AHEAD:** *This salad can be made up to one day in advance. Store, covered, in the refrigerator until ready to serve.*

# PANTRY QUINOA SALAD

*Quinoa is not a traditional Southern staple, but it should be. This high-protein, gluten-free grain cooks much like rice and has a texture similar to couscous. It makes a delicious and healthy base for a salad or side. This recipe comes from the kitchen of my friend Leslie Schilling. Leslie is a nutritionist and recommends this salad to her clients because it is filling and easy to prepare in advance.*

2 cups quinoa, cooked per package
    directions and chilled
1 (4.25-ounce) jar roasted red peppers,
    drained and coarsely chopped
2 (6-ounce) jars marinated artichoke
    hearts, drained and coarsely chopped
1/4 cup pitted Kalamata olives, drained
    and coarsely chopped

2 tablespoons red wine vinegar
1/3 cup olive oil
1 tablespoon dried oregano
1/2 cup crumbled feta cheese
Kosher salt and freshly ground black
    pepper

Place the prepared quinoa in a large bowl. Add the red peppers, artichokes, and olives, and toss to combine. Add the vinegar, oil, and oregano, and toss to coat. Add the feta, and toss to combine. Season with salt and pepper to taste. Cover and refrigerate until ready to serve. Serve chilled.

SERVES 6 TO 8.

**V VARIATION:** *I love quinoa because it is delicious with just about anything. Feel free to substitute your favorite ingredients. Capers would be a good substitute for the olives. Beans would be a hearty and tasty addition to the mix.*

**✔ DO-AHEAD:** *The quinoa can be made a few days ahead. Store covered in the refrigerator until ready to use.*

**▦ WEEKNIGHT CLASSIC**

# PESTO PASTA SALAD

*Pesto is probably my favorite condiment. It gives anything it touches a taste of summer, and since it freezes well, it can be used year-round. I add frozen green peas to this dish to give it extra flavor and a pop of color.*

1/2 cup Homemade Basil Pesto, (see below) or store-bought
1/2 cup mayonnaise
1/2 pound cavatappi pasta, cooked per package directions and chilled

1/4 cup grated Parmesan cheese
3/4 cup frozen peas, thawed
Kosher salt and freshly ground black pepper

In a large bowl whisk together the pesto and mayonnaise. Add the cooked pasta, Parmesan, and peas, and toss to coat. Season with salt and pepper to taste.

Cover and refrigerate until ready to serve. Serve chilled.

SERVES 6.

**COOKING TIP:** *Feel free to use whatever short pasta you have on hand.*

**WEEKNIGHT CLASSIC**

# HOMEMADE BASIL PESTO

2 cups fresh basil leaves, packed
1/3 cup pine nuts
3 cloves garlic, minced

1/2 cup olive oil
1/2 cup grated Parmesan cheese
Kosher salt and freshly ground black pepper

Place the basil and pine nuts in a food processor and pulse a few times. Add the garlic and pulse a few times more.
Slowly add the olive oil in a constant stream while the food processor is on.

Stop to scrape down the sides of the food processor with a rubber spatula. Add the Parmesan, and pulse again until blended. Add a pinch of salt and freshly ground black pepper to taste.

MAKES 1 CUP.

## DELICIOUS USES FOR PESTO

Pesto is a condiment that I always keep in my freezer. In the summer, I make a batch with basil from my garden and freeze it in ice cube trays so I always have just the right portion. In the winter, I use store-bought pesto and freeze the leftovers for another day. It can be used warm or cold.

### Five More Uses for Pesto

A warm pasta sauce

A non-tomato pizza sauce

Tossed with veggies

A garnish for soup

A spread for sandwiches

# SHRIMP REMOULADE SALAD

*Shrimp remoulade is one of those iconic New Orleans dishes I order on every trip to the Big Easy. My dressing is a bit milder than what you will find at some New Orleans restaurants, but I think it makes for a better main course salad or sandwich filling.*

2 pounds large shrimp (16/20 count), peeled and deveined, thawed if using frozen

1 lemon, cut into quarters

1 cup mayonnaise

3 tablespoons whole grain Dijon mustard

1 tablespoon white wine vinegar

1 tablespoon prepared horseradish

1 teaspoon freshly squeezed lemon juice

1 clove garlic, minced

1/2 teaspoon paprika

Kosher salt and freshly ground black pepper

1/4 cup finely diced red onion (1/2 small onion)

1/4 cup finely sliced celery (1 stalk)

Butter lettuce for serving, if desired

Bring a large pot of water to a boil over high heat. Add the shrimp and lemon wedges. Reduce the heat to medium and cook until the shrimp turn pink, 3 to 4 minutes. Drain, discard the lemon wedges, and run the shrimp under cold water to stop the cooking process. Place in a large bowl and refrigerate while making the dressing.

In a small bowl whisk together the mayonnaise, mustard, vinegar, horseradish, lemon juice, garlic, and paprika until well combined. Season with salt and pepper to taste.

Take the shrimp out of the refrigerator. Add the red onion and celery to the shrimp and toss to combine. Add the dressing and toss until well coated. Adjust seasonings as needed. Cover and refrigerate for at least 1 hour or until ready to serve. Serve chilled, over a bed of lettuce if desired.

**SERVES 4.**

**COOKING TIP:** *I like large pieces of shrimp in my salad, but if you prefer, you can cut the shrimp into smaller, bite-size pieces.*

**PANTRY SHORTCUT:** *Precooked shrimp (fresh or frozen) can be substituted. They just won't have the same lemony flavor as when cooked with lemon wedges.*

**WEEKNIGHT CLASSIC**

# SOUTHERN CHICKEN SALAD

*In the South, we like things sweet. The grapes in this mixture add a delicious touch of sweetness to a classic luncheon salad. Serve it with sweet tea for the perfect Southern light lunch.*

3 boneless, skinless chicken breasts
   (about 1 1/4 pounds)
1/2 cup mayonnaise
2 tablespoons sour cream
1 tablespoon freshly squeezed lemon
   juice

1/4 cup finely chopped celery (1 stalk)
1 cup red seedless grapes, halved
1/2 cup chopped pecans
Kosher salt and freshly ground black
   pepper

Bring a large pot of water to a boil over high heat. Add the chicken, and bring back to a boil. Lower the temperature to medium, and simmer until the chicken is cooked through, about 15 minutes. Drain well. When the chicken is cool enough to handle, shred it into bite-size pieces. Refrigerate until cool.

In a small bowl whisk together the mayonnaise, sour cream, and lemon juice until well combined. Place the chicken, celery, grapes, and pecans in a large bowl, and toss to combine. Add the dressing, and toss to coat. Season with salt and pepper to taste. Cover and refrigerate until ready to serve. Serve chilled.

**SERVES 6.**

**PANTRY SHORTCUT:** *4 cups store-bought rotisserie chicken (shredded) or leftover chicken can be used.*

**DO-AHEAD:** *This salad can be made up to one day in advance. Store covered in the refrigerator until ready to serve.*

**WEEKNIGHT CLASSIC**

# STRAWBERRY FIELDS SALAD

*The blush wine vinaigrette in this recipe is a homemade version of a popular store-bought dressing. Making homemade dressings is very simple since many dressings, like this one, use ingredients most people already have in their pantries.*

**BLUSH WINE VINAIGRETTE**

3 tablespoons red wine vinegar
2 tablespoons freshly squeezed lemon juice
2 tablespoons sugar
5 tablespoons vegetable oil
Kosher salt and freshly ground pepper

**SALAD**

6 cups mixed baby greens
1/2 pint fresh strawberries, hulled and thinly sliced
2/3 cup green or red grapes, halved
1/4 cup sliced almonds, toasted
1/4 cup crumbled blue cheese
Kosher salt and freshly ground pepper

**TO MAKE THE BLUSH WINE VINAIGRETTE:** In a small bowl whisk together the vinegar, lemon juice, and sugar until the sugar has dissolved. Slowly add the oil in a stream, whisking to emulsify. Season with salt and pepper to taste.

**TO MAKE THE SALAD:** In a large salad bowl toss together the lettuce greens, strawberries, grapes, almonds, and crumbled blue cheese. Add the dressing to taste and gently toss. Season with salt and pepper to taste.

**MAKES 6 APPETIZER OR SIDE SALADS.**

**COOKING TIP:** *Add sliced chicken or a salmon fillet and you have a complete meal.*

**V VARIATION:** *Mix and match this colorful salad using your favorite ingredients. Try substituting spinach or dried cranberries. Goat cheese is also a nice substitute for the blue cheese.*

**DO-AHEAD:** *The dressing can be made up to two days in advance. Store covered in the refrigerator until ready to use.*

**WEEKNIGHT CLASSIC**

# ROASTED SWEET POTATO SALAD WITH DRIED CRANBERRIES AND PECANS

*This colorful salad is a modern spin on potato salad. Using Southern staples like sweet potatoes and pecans, it's lighter than a classic potato salad since the dressing is simply lime juice rather than being mayonnaise or sour cream based.*

2 pounds sweet potatoes
   (3 or 4 medium), peeled and cut into
   3/4-inch cubes
2 tablespoons olive oil
1 tablespoon cumin
Kosher salt and freshly ground pepper

1/4 cup finely diced red onion
   (1/2 small onion)
1/2 cup dried cranberries
1/3 cup toasted chopped pecans
Juice of 1 lime
1/4 cup chopped fresh cilantro

Preheat the oven to 350 degrees.

In a large bowl toss the sweet potatoes with the olive oil and cumin. Season with salt and pepper to taste. On a baking sheet, evenly spread the potatoes in a single layer. Bake until the potatoes are cooked but still firm, 35 to 40 minutes. Refrigerate until cool.

Place the cooled sweet potatoes in a large bowl. Add the red onions, cranberries, and pecans, and toss to combine. Add the lime juice and fresh cilantro, and toss to combine. Season with salt and pepper to taste. Cover and refrigerate until ready to serve. Serve chilled.

SERVES 4.

**COOKING TIP:** *I like to line my baking sheets with parchment paper. The paper liner prevents sticking and helps make cleanup easier.*

**V VARIATION:** *Pine nuts would be a tasty substitute for the pecans.*

**DO-AHEAD:** *This salad can be made up to one day in advance. Add the fresh cilantro just before serving.*

# THREE-BEAN SALAD

*My good friend Lucia Heros is always whipping up something delicious. This salad is a prime example of what she can create with what she has on hand.*

1 (15-ounce) can garbanzo beans, rinsed and drained

1 (15-ounce) can dark-red kidney beans, rinsed and drained

1 (15-ounce) can pinto beans, rinsed and drained

1/2 cup finely diced green bell pepper (1 small pepper)

1 cup cherry tomatoes, halved

1/4 cup thinly sliced yellow onions (1/2 small onion)

1/4 cup chopped fresh flat-leaf parsley

1/4 cup olive oil

3 tablespoons balsamic vinegar

Zest of 1 lemon

2 tablespoons freshly squeezed lemon juice

2 tablespoons orange juice

Dash of hot sauce

Kosher salt and freshly ground black pepper

In a large bowl place the garbanzo beans, kidney beans, pinto beans, green pepper, tomatoes, onions, and parsley, and toss to combine.

In a small bowl whisk together the olive oil, balsamic vinegar, lemon zest, lemon juice, orange juice, and hot sauce. Add to the bean mixture, and toss to coat. Season with salt and pepper to taste. Cover and refrigerate until ready to serve. Serve chilled.

**SERVES 6.**

**COOKING TIP:** *If you would like a little more heat in this salad, add some extra hot sauce.*

**PANTRY SHORTCUT:** *Fresh-squeezed juices are always best, but I often turn to the store-bought bottle of OJ I have in the fridge when whipping up dishes like this.*

**DO-AHEAD:** *This salad can be made up to one day in advance. Store in the refrigerator until ready to serve.*

**WEEKNIGHT CLASSIC**

# JELLY JAR SALAD DRESSING

*My good friend Margaret Fraser has come up with the best way to use that almost-empty jar of jelly. You can enjoy the last flavor from a jar, and since you mix it in the almost-empty jar, it comes together quickly with hardly any cleanup. My kids enjoy the sweetness that jelly gives a classic vinaigrette, so I often whip this up even when I only have full jars of jelly in the fridge!*

1/4 cup white wine vinegar
1 almost empty jar of jelly
   (about 2 tablespoons)
1/3 cup extra-virgin olive oil

1 clove garlic, minced
1/2 teaspoon Dijon mustard
Kosher salt and freshly ground black
   pepper

Place the vinegar in the almost empty jelly jar and shake well. Add the olive oil, garlic, and mustard, and shake again until well combined. Season with salt and pepper to taste.

SERVES 4 TO 6.

**COOKING TIP:** *Margaret's favorite jellies to use are raspberry, cherry, and strawberry. I like it with apricot too. Her kids love it with grape jelly. You can even try it with spicier jellies, like ginger or hot pepper, for a vinaigrette with a kick.*

**DO-AHEAD:** *Salad dressings can be made up to two days in advance. Store covered in the refrigerator until ready to serve. If the oil has congealed or the dressing separated, let the mixture come to room temperature and shake well before serving.*

# SOUPS

comforting.

After I had my first baby, a friend brought me a huge mason jar full of potato soup and a pan of cornbread. I think that was just about my favorite gift I received. This simple meal was the perfect food for a tired and overwhelmed new mother. Since then it has become my gift-of-choice for friends who have a new one at home or who have been sick.

Soup has also become my go-to lunch. I make a big batch and freeze it in individual portions. That way I can always have a bowl of my favorite soup whenever I want. Plus, it's an easy and filling dish for my husband to take to work for lunch. If you went to my freezer right now, you'd be sure to find a few containers of Creamy Tomato Soup (page 52), White Bean and Country Ham Soup (page 67), and Freezer Veggie Soup (page 56).

# BROCCOLI AND CHEDDAR SOUP

*Some broccoli soups are more like chowders, with added ingredients like potatoes and carrots. I prefer my broccoli and cheese soup to be simple and creamy, like this version, where the broccoli takes center stage.*

4 tablespoons unsalted butter, divided
¼ cup finely diced yellow onion
   (½ small onion)
1 clove garlic, minced
2 cups chicken stock
2 tablespoons all-purpose flour
1 cup 2% milk
2 cups shredded sharp Cheddar cheese

½ teaspoon ground dry mustard
¼ teaspoon paprika
Kosher salt and freshly ground black
   pepper
1 (10-ounce) package frozen broccoli
   spears, thawed and coarsely
   chopped into bite-size pieces

In a large stockpot or Dutch oven over medium-high heat, melt 2 tablespoons of the butter. Add the onion, and cook, stirring frequently, until soft, about 5 minutes. Add the garlic, and cook until fragrant, about 1 more minute. Add the stock, and lower the temperature to medium-low. Let simmer while making the cream sauce.

In a medium saucepan over medium-low heat, melt the remaining 2 tablespoons of butter. When the butter starts to foam, add the flour and cook, whisking, until thickened, about 1 minute. While continuing to whisk, gradually add the milk. Over medium-high heat, bring the mixture to a boil. Reduce the heat to medium-low, and simmer, whisking constantly, until the mixture thickens, 5 to 8 minutes.

Add the cream sauce to the stock mixture, and whisk to combine. Add the cheese, and whisk until melted and smooth. Stir in the dry mustard and paprika. Season with salt and pepper to taste. Add the broccoli, and stir to combine. Bring the mixture to a boil over high heat. Reduce the heat to medium-low, and simmer uncovered, stirring occasionally, until the broccoli is tender and the flavors have melded, about 15 minutes. Serve warm.

SERVES 4.

**COOKING TIP:** *This soup thickens as it cools. If it is too thick, add a little more stock or milk.*

**V VARIATION:** *If using fresh broccoli, you should precook it until just fork-tender, about 5 minutes, before adding it to this soup. Otherwise it may not be tender enough. Do not overcook it, though.*

**WEEKNIGHT CLASSIC**

# CHICKEN AND RICE SOUP

*Forget the noodles! In my house, we prefer our chicken soup with rice!*

2 split bone-in, skin-on chicken breasts
(about 1 3/4 pounds)
Kosher salt and freshly ground black
pepper
1 tablespoon olive oil
1/2 cup finely diced yellow onion
(1 small onion)

1/2 cup thinly sliced celery (2 stalks)
1/2 cup finely diced carrots (2 carrots)
1 bay leaf
1 teaspoon dried rosemary
8 cups chicken stock
4 cups cooked white rice

Rinse the chicken and pat dry with paper towels. Generously season the chicken with salt and pepper. In a large stockpot or Dutch oven over medium-high heat, warm the oil until a few droplets of water sizzle when carefully sprinkled in the pot. Add the chicken, and sear until golden brown on both sides, about 6 minutes. Transfer the chicken to a plate.

Drain all but about 1 tablespoon of fat from the pot. Add the onion, celery, carrots, bay leaf, and rosemary. Cook, stirring often, until soft, about 5 minutes. Add the stock, and return the chicken to the pot. Bring the mixture to a boil over high heat. Reduce the heat to medium-low, and simmer until the chicken is tender and cooked through, about 45 minutes.

Using a slotted spoon, transfer the cooked chicken to a large bowl to cool. Keep the broth warm in the pot. Once the chicken is cool enough to handle, remove the meat from the bones and discard the skin. Shred the chicken into 2-inch pieces.

Season the broth with salt and pepper to taste. Discard the bay leaf. Return the chicken to the pot, and reheat the soup until the chicken is warmed through. Stir in the cooked rice. Serve warm.

SERVES 6.

**V** **VARIATION:** *This soup is also delicious with noodles in place of the rice.*

**FREEZES WELL:** *If possible, it is best to freeze the soup without the rice because the rice will absorb the broth and become mushy. When the soup is thawed, simply add freshly cooked rice.*

# CREAMY TOMATO SOUP

*A steamy bowl of creamy tomato soup and a warm grilled cheese sandwich is a marriage made in heaven. Instead of serving the sandwich on the side, try cutting it up and using the cheesy squares as croutons!*

2 tablespoons olive oil
1/4 cup finely diced yellow onion
   (1/2 small onion)
2 cloves garlic, minced
1 (28-ounce) can crushed tomatoes
1/2 teaspoon dried oregano

1/4 teaspoon dried thyme leaves
1 tablespoon sugar
3 cups chicken stock
1 cup heavy cream
Kosher salt and freshly ground black
   pepper

In a large stockpot over medium-high heat, warm the oil until a few droplets of water sizzle when carefully sprinkled in the pot. Add the onion and garlic. Cook, stirring often, until the onions are soft, about 5 minutes.

Add the tomatoes, oregano, thyme, and sugar, and stir to combine. Pour in the chicken stock and stir to combine. Bring the mixture to a boil over high heat. Lower the heat to medium-low and simmer uncovered until the soup has thickened, about 20 minutes. Whisk in the heavy cream and simmer for 10 more minutes. Season with salt and pepper to taste. Serve warm.

SERVES 4 TO 6.

**COOKING TIP:** *The sugar in this recipe helps balance the acidity of the canned tomatoes.*

**FREEZES WELL**

**WEEKNIGHT CLASSIC**

# CREAMY VIDALIA ONION SOUP

*The key to a good onion soup is making sure that the onions are well caramelized. I guarantee it is worth the wait!*

6 tablespoons unsalted butter, divided
6 cups thinly sliced Vidalia or other
    sweet yellow onions (4 large onions)
2 cloves garlic, minced
2 bay leaves
1/2 teaspoon dried thyme leaves
2 tablespoons all-purpose flour

8 cups chicken stock
1 cup heavy cream
Kosher salt and freshly ground black
    pepper
1/2 small loaf French or Italian country
    bread, cut into 1-inch cubes (2 cups)
2 tablespoons grated Parmesan cheese

In a large stockpot or Dutch oven over medium heat, melt 3 tablespoons of butter. Add the onion, garlic, bay leaves, and thyme, and cook, stirring often, until soft and caramel colored, about 45 minutes.

Dust the onion mixture with the flour, and stir to coat. Cook, stirring, about 1 minute.

Pour in the stock, and bring the mixture to a boil over high heat. Lower the temperature to medium, and simmer uncovered until the flavors have melded, about 25 minutes. Add the heavy cream and simmer uncovered for 10 minutes. Discard the bay leaves. Using an immersion blender or a regular blender, puree the soup until smooth. Season with salt and pepper to taste.

Preheat the oven to 400 degrees. Melt the remaining 3 tablespoons of butter. Place the bread on a rimmed baking sheet, and toss with the melted butter and Parmesan. Bake until golden and crisp, about 6 minutes.

Serve warm with the croutons on top.

SERVES 6.

**COOKING TIP:** *For a classic French onion soup, just omit the cream and do not puree the soup. Top with croutons and a slice of Gruyère or Swiss cheese.*

# FREEZER VEGGIE SOUP

*My friend Nevada Presley runs a vegetarian prepared-foods business called Get Fresh Memphis. All her healthy options are yummy, but her soups are some of my favorite things to order. They are always simple, uncomplicated, and delicious. I whip up this one on days when I feel like a quick and healthy meal.*

2 tablespoons olive oil
1/2 cup finely diced yellow onion
   (1 small onion)
4 cloves garlic, minced
1 (14.5-ounce) can Italian-style diced tomatoes
4 cups vegetable broth
1 (12-ounce) bag frozen mixed
   vegetables, thawed (about 3 cups)

2 cups frozen cut okra, thawed and
   rinsed
1 (14.5-ounce) can cannellini beans,
   drained and rinsed
Kosher salt and freshly ground black
   pepper

In a large stockpot over medium-high heat, warm the oil until a few droplets of water sizzle when carefully sprinkled in the pot. Add the onion, and cook, stirring often, until the onions are soft, about 5 minutes. Add the garlic, and cook until fragrant, about 1 minute more. Add the tomatoes, broth, mixed vegetables, okra, and beans. Bring the mixture to a boil over high heat. Lower the heat to medium-low, and simmer uncovered until the vegetables are tender, about 20 minutes. Season with salt and pepper to taste. Serve warm.

**SERVES 4 TO 6.**

➤➤ **PANTRY SHORTCUTS:** *Italian-style diced tomatoes are simply diced tomatoes flavored with Italian seasonings. If you don't have a can in your pantry, use regular diced tomatoes plus 1 tablespoon of dried Italian seasoning.*

*A bag of frozen mixed vegetables contains carrots, corn, green beans, and green peas. You can always add whatever frozen vegetables you have on hand. You can also substitute chicken stock for the vegetable broth.*

❄ **FREEZES WELL**

▦ **WEEKNIGHT CLASSIC**

# FROGMORE STEW

*Frogmore stew is the low-country version of a shrimp boil. Often served rustically with peel-on shrimp and corn on the cob, this more refined version from Ryan Trimm, chef and owner of the renowned Sweetgrass in Memphis, Tennessee, is perfect for your dinner table.*

1 cup small red potatoes, scrubbed and cut into 1-inch pieces
2 tablespoons olive oil, divided
1/3 pound smoked sausage, cut into 1/4-inch slices (about 1 cup)
1/2 cup thinly sliced yellow onion (1 small onion)
3/4 pound large shrimp (16/20 count), peeled and deveined, thawed if using frozen

4 cups chicken stock
1 cup corn kernels, thawed if using frozen
3/4 cup diced tomatoes, drained if using canned
1/2 teaspoon dried thyme leaves
Kosher salt and freshly ground black pepper

Put the potatoes in a medium pot, and cover with cold water by 1 inch. Bring to a boil over high heat, and then lower the temperature to a simmer. Cook just until the potatoes are par-cooked and still very firm, 3 to 4 minutes. Drain and set aside.

In a large stockpot or Dutch oven over medium-high heat, warm 1 tablespoon oil until a few droplets of water sizzle when carefully sprinkled in the pot. Add the sausage, and cook until browned, 4 to 5 minutes. Transfer the sausage to a plate and reserve.

Add the remaining 1 tablespoon oil to the pot. Add the onion, and cook over medium heat until soft, 3 to 5 minutes. Add the potatoes, sausage, and shrimp, and cook about 1 minute more. Add the stock, corn, tomatoes, and thyme. Stir to combine. Season with salt and pepper to taste. Bring the mixture to a boil over high heat. Reduce the heat to medium-low, and simmer uncovered, stirring occasionally, until the flavors have melded, about 20 minutes. Adjust seasonings as needed. Serve warm.

SERVES 4.

**COOKING TIP:** *Any type of smoked sausage would work in this dish. Ryan uses a sweet fennel sausage at his restaurant.*

WEEKNIGHT CLASSIC

# LUCKY BLACK-EYED PEA AND COLLARD GREEN SOUP

*Since I can use good luck and good fortune anytime, I decided to combine these two lucky New Year's ingredients into one dish that can be enjoyed year-round. This soup pairs these lucky foods with vegetables and smoky bacon for a dish that is hearty and satisfying.*

4 slices bacon, cut into ¼-inch pieces
½ cup finely diced yellow onion
   (1 small onion)
¼ cup thinly sliced celery (1 stalk)
½ cup thinly sliced carrots (2 carrots)
2 cloves garlic, minced
½ teaspoon dried thyme leaves
1 (14.5-ounce) can diced tomatoes

6 cups chicken stock
2 (15-ounce) cans black-eyed peas,
   drained and rinsed
1 cup thinly sliced collard greens, tough
   stems and ribs removed if using
   fresh, or thawed if using frozen
Kosher salt and freshly ground black
   pepper

Place the bacon in a large stockpot or Dutch oven, and cook over medium heat until crispy, 3 to 4 minutes. Add the onion, celery, carrots, garlic, and thyme. Cook, stirring, until the onions are soft, about 5 minutes.

Add the tomatoes, stock, black-eyed peas, and collard greens, and stir to combine. Season with salt and pepper to taste. Bring the mixture to a boil over high heat. Reduce the heat to medium-low, cover, and simmer until the collard greens are tender and the flavors have melded, about 20 minutes. Adjust seasonings as needed. Serve warm.

**SERVES 6.**

⟫ **PANTRY SHORTCUT:** *Frozen spinach leaves or kale can be used in place of the collard greens.*

Ⓥ **VARIATION:** *For a vegetarian version, omit the bacon and sauté the vegetables in olive oil instead.*

❄ **FREEZES WELL**

▦ **WEEKNIGHT CLASSIC**

# LOADED POTATO SOUP

*I garnish my potato soup just as I would my baked potatoes—loaded with crispy bacon, shredded cheese, and scallions.*

2 tablespoons unsalted butter
1/2 cup finely diced yellow onion
    (1 small onion)
2 pounds small red potatoes, peeled
    and cut into 1-inch pieces
4 cups chicken stock
1 cup heavy cream

Kosher salt and freshly ground black
    pepper
1/2 cup crumbled cooked bacon
    (about 6 slices)
1/2 cup shredded Cheddar cheese
2 tablespoons thinly sliced scallions or
    chives, optional

In a large Dutch oven or stockpot over medium-high heat, melt the butter. Add the onion, and cook until soft, about 5 minutes. Add the potatoes and stock.

Bring the mixture to a boil over high heat. Lower the temperature to medium, and simmer uncovered until the potatoes are tender, about 10 minutes. Stir in the heavy cream, and cook for 5 more minutes.

Place half the soup in a blender or food processor, and puree until smooth. Add the pureed soup back to the pot, and stir to combine. Season with salt and pepper to taste. Serve warm, garnished with crumbled bacon, cheese, and scallions or chives if desired.

SERVES 6.

**COOKING TIP:** *If the soup is too thick, you can thin it by adding a little more chicken stock or milk.*

**PANTRY SHORTCUT:** *Frozen Southern-style hash brown potatoes are the ideal shortcut for this recipe. No need to peel or dice potatoes—just pour them straight into the soup pot from the bag.*

**WEEKNIGHT CLASSIC**

# SWEET CORNBREAD AND BUTTERMILK SOUP

*When I first tasted this soup at Paradise Café in Memphis, Tennessee, I wanted the recipe. This silky soup has a lightly tangy buttermilk flavor that is perfectly contrasted by the sweet cornbread croutons floating on top. Thank you, Bob and Betty Sternburgh, for graciously sharing the recipe.*

4 cups chicken stock
¹/₄ cup thinly sliced celery (1 stalk)
¹/₄ cup finely diced yellow onion
   (¹/₂ small onion)
³/₄ cup corn kernels, thawed if using frozen
4 tablespoons cornstarch

4 tablespoons water
¹/₂ cup sour cream
1 cup buttermilk
Kosher salt and freshly ground pepper
1 pan Skillet Cornbread (see page 176
   for recipe), cut into 1-inch pieces

▒ In a large stockpot or Dutch oven, place the stock, celery, onion, and corn. Bring to a boil over high heat. Lower the temperature to medium, and simmer uncovered until the flavors have melded, about 10 minutes.

▒ In a small bowl whisk together the cornstarch and water. Add the cornstarch mixture to the soup, and cook, whisking constantly, over medium heat until thickened to the consistency of pancake batter, about 3 minutes. Add the sour cream and buttermilk, and whisk to combine. Remove from the heat, and season with salt and pepper to taste.

▒ To serve, ladle the warm soup into bowls and place several pieces of cornbread on top.

**SERVES 6.**

🍴 **COOKING TIP:** *A slurry made with cornstarch and water is a simple way to thicken just about any sauce. The rule of thumb is for each cup of sauce you would like to thicken, mix 1 tablespoon of cornstarch with 1 tablespoon of cold water. The major difference between a slurry and a roux is that a roux is begun at the start of cooking the dish while a slurry is added at the end.*

 **WEEKNIGHT CLASSIC**

# WHITE BEAN AND COUNTRY HAM SOUP

*This hearty soup is a quick and delicious dish that is great for either lunch or dinner. I serve it with a small salad and a piece of cornbread for a satisfying supper.*

1 tablespoon olive oil
1/2 cup finely diced yellow onion
   (1 small onion)
1 cup thinly sliced carrots (4 carrots)
1/3 cup thinly sliced celery (1 to 2 stalks)
1 cup finely diced country ham
1 clove garlic, minced
4 cups chicken stock

4 (15-ounce) cans white cannellini beans
   or white navy beans, drained and
   rinsed
1 teaspoon dried thyme leaves
1 bay leaf
Kosher salt and freshly ground black
   pepper

In a large stockpot or Dutch oven over medium-high heat, warm the oil until a few droplets of water sizzle when carefully sprinkled in the pot. Add the onion, carrots, and celery, and cook until soft, about 5 minutes. Add the ham and garlic, and cook until the garlic is fragrant, about 1 minute more.

Add the stock, beans, thyme, and bay leaf. Stir to combine. Season with salt and pepper to taste. Bring the mixture to a boil over high heat. Reduce the heat to medium-low, and simmer uncovered, stirring occasionally, until thickened, 45 to 50 minutes. Adjust seasonings as needed, and remove bay leaf. Serve warm.

**SERVES 6.**

**COOKING TIP:** *Be careful when seasoning this soup with salt. The country ham is naturally pretty salty, so be sure to taste the soup before adding more salt.*

**FREEZES WELL**

# CHICKEN

EVERYBODY LOVES CHICKEN. I WOULD EVEN VENTURE TO SAY THAT IT'S probably America's favorite meat.

What I love about this bird is its versatility. With such a neutral flavor, it can be paired with myriad ingredients and cooked a multitude of ways to create an infinite number of different dishes. I could serve chicken every night if I wanted to, and my family would never say, "Chicken again?!"

In this chapter I try to show the many ways that chicken can be prepared—all with a Southern twist, of course!

Fried chicken is a Southern classic, but to be honest, classic fried chicken is not the easiest dish to master, plus so many restaurants do it so well. Instead, I chose to share with you my Peanut-y Fried Chicken Strips (page 86). Since they are part-fried and part-baked, they take the guesswork out of frying chicken.

My family loves chicken pot pie and biscuits. I often combine the two for a new twist on a classic (page 76). After writing my last book, *Simply Grilling*, I am always on the lookout for tasty new grilled chicken dishes. Grilled Chicken with Peach Barbecue Sauce (page 78) and Mimi and Pop's Marinated Grilled Chicken (page 88) may just become two of your new grill go-tos.

Dishes like Pa's Herbed Chicken Parts (page 84) and Lemony Chicken (page 83) make frequent appearances on our dinner table on busy weeknights.

Whether it's grilled, fried, sautéed, baked, or roasted, I think you'll agree that chicken makes a delicious and easy option for supper.

# BRAISED CHICKEN WITH MUSHROOMS AND GRITS

*Braising is an almost foolproof way to cook dinner. It is a classic cooking technique where the main ingredient is first browned in butter or oil, and then simmered in liquid over low heat in a covered pan. When done with flavorful liquids (like stock or wine) and some added seasonings, braising offers more flavor than boiling and doesn't dry out food like roasting can.*

4 boneless, skinless chicken breasts
(about 1 1/2 pounds)
Kosher salt
Freshly ground pepper
2 tablespoons olive oil, divided
1 pound white button mushrooms,
wiped clean and thinly sliced

2 cloves garlic, minced
1 1/2 cups chicken stock
4 cups Creamy Stone-Ground Grits
(see page 162 for the recipe), warm
2 tablespoons chopped fresh parsley,
optional garnish

▧ Rinse the chicken and pat dry with paper towels. Generously season with salt and pepper. In a large skillet over medium-high heat, warm 1 tablespoon of oil until a few droplets of water sizzle when carefully sprinkled in the pan. Cook the chicken until nicely browned on both sides, about 3 minutes per side. Transfer the chicken to a plate and reserve.

▧ Add the remaining 1 tablespoon of oil to the skillet. Add the mushrooms and garlic. Season with salt and pepper to taste. Cover and cook over medium heat until the mushrooms release their juices, 2 to 3 minutes. Remove the lid. Raise the heat to medium-high and cook, stirring occasionally, until the mushrooms are golden, about 5 minutes.

▧ Add the stock. Cook until the mushrooms are tender and the liquid is reduced, 8 to 10 minutes.

▧ Return the chicken to the skillet. Cover, reduce the heat to low, and simmer until the chicken is cooked through, 10 to 12 minutes.

▧ To serve, portion the warm grits into the serving bowls and place a chicken breast over the grits. Pour the sauce over the chicken and serve hot. Garnish with chopped parsley if desired.

SERVES 4.

👍 **COOKING TIP:** *Be sure to take an extra 2 to 3 minutes to cook the mushrooms covered before browning them. This simple step to release the juices will help you have more tender mushrooms.*

📅 WEEKNIGHT CLASSIC

# CHICKEN DIVAN

*Casseroles are perfect for feeding a crowd, and this cozy one will please everyone at your table. I give it a fun spin by topping it with crushed potato chips instead of the traditional bread crumb coating.*

2 (10-ounce) packages frozen broccoli
   spears, thawed
4 cups cooked, shredded chicken
   (about 3 skinless, boneless breasts)
4 tablespoons unsalted butter, divided
1 cup sliced mushrooms (4 ounces)
2 tablespoons all-purpose flour
1/2 cup 2% or whole milk

1/2 cup chicken stock
1 cup shredded sharp Cheddar cheese
1/2 cup mayonnaise
1/2 cup sour cream
1 teaspoon curry powder
Kosher salt and freshly ground pepper
1 cup crushed potato chips

Preheat the oven to 350 degrees.

Cook the broccoli according to the package directions. Drain and place in a 9 x 13-inch baking dish. Evenly scatter the cooked chicken over the top of the broccoli.

In a medium saucepan over medium heat, melt 2 tablespoons of butter. Add the mushrooms and cook until golden brown, 4 to 5 minutes. Transfer the mushrooms to a plate and reserve.

Add the remaining 2 tablespoons butter to the same pan and heat over medium-low. When the butter starts to foam, add the flour and cook, whisking, until golden brown, 2 to 3 minutes. While continuing to whisk, gradually add the milk and chicken stock. Bring the mixture to a boil over medium-high heat. Reduce the heat to medium-low and simmer, whisking constantly, until the mixture thickens, 5 to 8 minutes.

Add the cheese and stir until melted. Remove from the heat and stir in the mushrooms, mayonnaise, sour cream, and curry powder. Season with salt and pepper to taste.

Pour the mixture evenly over the top of the chicken. Spread the crushed potato chips evenly over the top of the casserole.

Bake until golden brown and bubbly, 30 to 35 minutes. Serve warm.

SERVES 6.

**PANTRY SHORTCUTS:** *If you don't have chips on hand, mix 1 cup panko bread crumbs and 2 tablespoons melted butter to make a similar topping.*

*I like to make my sauces from scratch, but a can of cream of mushroom soup can be substituted for the base of the homemade cream sauce. Just omit the mixture made with the mushrooms, butter, flour, milk, and chicken stock. Instead, warm the condensed soup in a saucepan and then stir in the Cheddar cheese.*

**FREEZES WELL**

# CHICKEN FRICASSEE

*A fricassee is a French dish of braised cut-up chicken. Some versions have a white sauce, whereas others, like this Creole version from my grandmother's kitchen, have a tomato sauce. The classic recipe calls for using a whole chicken cut into pieces. For convenience, I usually just pick up a package of chicken thighs at my local market.*

3 pounds bone-in, skin-on chicken thighs
Kosher salt and freshly ground black
   pepper
2 tablespoons olive oil
1 cup diced yellow onion (1 large onion)
3/4 cup diced green bell pepper
   (1 large pepper)

1/4 cup thinly sliced celery (1 stalk)
1 tablespoon dried oregano
1 tablespoon dried thyme leaves
1 (28-ounce) can diced tomatoes
4 cups water
2 bay leaves

Rinse the chicken, and pat dry with paper towels. Generously season the chicken with salt and pepper. In a large stockpot or Dutch oven over medium-high heat, warm the oil until a few droplets of water sizzle when carefully sprinkled in the pot. Cook the chicken, stirring occasionally, until nicely browned, about 5 minutes. Transfer the chicken to a plate. Drain all but about 1 tablespoon of fat from the pot.

To the pot add the onion, green pepper, celery, oregano, and thyme, and cook, stirring often, until soft, about 10 minutes. Add the tomatoes, water, and bay leaves. Season with salt and pepper to taste. Return the chicken to the pot. Bring the sauce to a boil over high heat, lower the heat to medium-low, and simmer, covered, until the chicken is tender and falls off the bone, about 1 1/2 hours. Serve warm.

SERVES 6.

**COOKING TIP:** *If using a whole chicken, buying a whole chicken and cutting it up yourself is cheaper than buying an already butchered bird.*

**FREEZES WELL**

# CHICKEN POT PIE WITH BUTTERMILK-HERB BISCUITS

(PHOTO ON PAGE 68)

*Nothing says comfort food like chicken pot pie. Chicken and vegetables in a rich and creamy sauce topped with flavorful biscuits makes for a satisfying one-dish meal.*

### POT PIE FILLING

3 cups water
1 cup peeled and finely sliced carrots
   (4 carrots)
1 cup peeled and diced white potatoes
   (1 large potato)
1/2 cup finely diced yellow onion
   (1 small onion)
1 cup green peas, thawed if using frozen
4 boneless, skinless chicken breasts
   (about 1 1/2 pounds)
Kosher salt and freshly ground black
   pepper
2 tablespoons olive oil
4 tablespoons unsalted butter

4 tablespoons all-purpose flour
2 cups 2% or whole milk
2 cups chicken stock
1 teaspoon dried thyme leaves

### BUTTERMILK-HERB BISCUITS

1 1/2 cups all-purpose flour
1 1/2 teaspoons baking powder
1/2 teaspoon baking soda
1/4 teaspoon salt
1/4 cup cold unsalted butter, cut into
   pea-size pieces
1 cup buttermilk
1 tablespoon dried rosemary

▪ Preheat the oven to 400 degrees.

▪ **TO PREPARE THE POT PIE FILLING:**
Fill a medium saucepan with the water
and bring to a boil over high heat. Add the
carrots, potato, onion, and peas and cook
until crisp-tender, about 8 minutes. Drain
well and set aside.

▪ While the vegetables are cooking, rinse
the chicken and pat dry with paper towels.
Cut into bite-size pieces and generously
season with salt and pepper. In a Dutch
oven or large saucepan over medium-high

heat, warm the oil until a few droplets of
water sizzle when carefully sprinkled in
the pan. Cook the chicken until nicely
browned on all sides, about 5 minutes.
Transfer the chicken to a plate and reserve.

▪ Add the butter to the pan and melt
over medium-low heat. Add the flour and
whisk until the mixture is golden brown, 4
to 5 minutes. While continuing to whisk,
gradually add the milk and stock. Add the
thyme and season with salt and pepper
to taste. Bring the mixture to a boil over

medium-high heat. Reduce the heat to medium-low and simmer, whisking constantly, until the mixture thickens, 5 to 8 minutes. Add the chicken, carrots, potato, onion, and peas. Stir to combine. Adjust the seasonings as necessary. Pour the filling into a 9 x 13-inch baking dish.

▦ **TO PREPARE THE BISCUITS:** In the bowl of an electric mixer fitted with the paddle attachment, combine the flour, baking powder, baking soda, and salt. With the mixer on low, add the butter and mix until coarse crumbs form, 30 to 45 seconds. Slowly add the buttermilk and rosemary to the flour mixture and mix only until the dough just comes together.

▦ Drop spoonfuls of the biscuit dough evenly across the top of the filling.

▦ Bake until golden brown and bubbling, 35 to 30 minutes.

SERVES 8.

 🔥 **COOKING TIP:** *Sometimes I top the filling with piecrust rather than biscuits for a more traditional pot pie. This filling works well with either topping. When you are using piecrust, you need to add about 10 minutes to the cooking time.*

» **PANTRY SHORTCUT:** *Short on time? Pick up a rotisserie chicken at your local grocery store for this recipe. For another shortcut, you can use canned biscuits, but I much prefer homemade.*

✔ **DO-AHEAD:** *Pot pie filling can be made a day in advance. It also freezes well unbaked. Wait to make the biscuit dough until just before baking.*

❄ **FREEZES WELL**

# GRILLED CHICKEN WITH PEACH BARBECUE SAUCE

*Southern peaches add a delicious sweetness to just about anything ... including barbecue sauce! The key to perfect barbecue chicken is to apply the sauce when the chicken is almost done. This prevents the sauce from burning.*

### PEACH BARBECUE SAUCE
1 cup sliced peaches, thawed if using frozen
2 cups ketchup
1/2 cup water
1/3 cup cider vinegar
2 tablespoons light brown sugar
2 tablespoons molasses
1 teaspoon crushed red pepper flakes
1 teaspoon onion powder
1 teaspoon ground dry mustard
1 tablespoon Worcestershire sauce

### BARBECUE CHICKEN
Vegetable oil, for grates
4 boneless, skinless chicken breasts (about 1 1/2 pounds)
Kosher salt and freshly ground black pepper

■ **TO PREPARE THE BARBECUE SAUCE:** Put the peaches in a food processor and puree until smooth with some small chunks.

■ In a large saucepan combine the ketchup, water, cider vinegar, brown sugar, molasses, red pepper flakes, onion powder, dry mustard, and Worcestershire. Bring the sauce to a boil over high heat. Reduce the heat to medium-low and simmer, stirring occasionally, until the sauce thickens, 20 to 25 minutes. Stir in the reserved peach puree and cook until the flavors have melded, about 5 more minutes. Measure out 1 cup of sauce. Refrigerate the remaining sauce for another time. (It will keep for up to 5 days in your refrigerator.)

■ **TO PREPARE THE CHICKEN:** Preheat a clean grill to medium-high with the lid closed for 8 to 10 minutes. Lightly brush the grates with oil.

■ Generously season the chicken with the salt and pepper. Place the chicken on the grill. Close the lid and cook, turning

once, until no longer pink in the middle, 6 to 8 minutes per side. During the final 5 minutes of cooking, baste the chicken with the barbecue sauce. Remove the chicken from the grill. Serve warm.

SERVES 4.

**COOKING TIP:** *Boneless, skinless chicken breasts can also be easily grilled indoors on a grill pan.*

**DO-AHEAD:** *The Peach Barbecue Sauce can be made up to 5 days in advance. Store covered in your refrigerator.*

**PANTRY SHORTCUT:** *Making a homemade barbecue sauce is very easy, but it does take time. You can stir the pureed peaches into your favorite bottled barbecue sauce if you prefer. Just simmer for 5 minutes to meld the flavors.*

**WEEKNIGHT CLASSIC**

# KING RANCH CHICKEN

*This spicy chicken casserole is perfect for feeding a group. I like to serve it with a dollop of sour cream on top.*

2 tablespoons unsalted butter
1/2 cup diced yellow onion (1 small onion)
1/2 cup diced green bell pepper (1 small pepper)
3 cloves garlic, minced
2 tablespoons all-purpose flour
2 teaspoons chili powder
1/2 teaspoon cumin
1/4 teaspoon cayenne pepper
1 cup chicken stock
1/2 cup 2% or whole milk

1 (14.5-ounce) can diced tomatoes, drained
1 (4-ounce) can diced green chilies
1/3 cup sour cream
Kosher salt and freshly ground black pepper
12 (6-inch) corn tortillas, cut into 1/2-inch strips
4 cups cooked, shredded chicken (about 3 skinless, boneless breasts)
3 cups shredded sharp Cheddar cheese

▩ Preheat the oven to 350 degrees.

▩ In a Dutch oven or large stockpot melt the butter over medium-high heat. Add the onion and green pepper and cook until soft, about 5 minutes. Add the garlic and cook until fragrant, about 1 more minute.

▩ Dust the vegetables with the flour and stir to coat. Add the chili powder, cumin, and cayenne pepper. Cook for 1 minute.

▩ Add the stock and cook on medium-low heat, stirring, until the mixture starts to thicken, 5 to 7 minutes. Stir in the milk, tomatoes, and green chilies. Cover the pot and cook, stirring occasionally, until the flavors have melded, about 15 minutes.

Remove the pot from the heat and stir in the sour cream. Season with salt and pepper to taste.

▩ Spoon 1/2 cup of the sauce evenly onto the bottom of a 9 x 13-inch baking dish. Layer half of the tortilla strips over the sauce. Evenly place half of the chicken over the tortillas. Spoon half of the remaining sauce evenly over the top of the chicken. Sprinkle 1 1/2 cups of cheese evenly over the sauce. Repeat the layering of the tortilla strips, chicken, sauce, and cheese with the remaining ingredients.

▩ Bake until golden brown and bubbly, 30 to 35 minutes. Serve warm.

SERVES 6 TO 8.

**PANTRY SHORTCUT:** *2 (10-ounce) cans tomatoes with green chilies can be substituted for the individual cans of diced tomatoes and green chilies.*

**FREEZES WELL:** *Freeze unbaked casserole for up to one month. Thaw in the refrigerator overnight before baking.*

# LEMONY CHICKEN

*This lemony chicken dish is my Southern spin on an Italian piccata. Serve with rice or angel hair pasta for a fabulous meal.*

4 boneless, skinless chicken breasts
    (about 1 1/2 pounds)
Kosher salt and freshly ground pepper
1/3 cup all-purpose flour
2 tablespoons olive oil

3/4 cup chicken stock
3/4 cup freshly squeezed lemon juice
3 tablespoons unsalted butter
1 lemon, thinly sliced into rounds

Rinse the chicken and pat dry with paper towels. Place the chicken in between 2 pieces of wax paper or plastic wrap, and using a meat mallet or rolling pin, pound to 1/4 inch thick. Generously season both sides of the chicken breasts with salt and pepper. Place the flour in a shallow bowl and lightly dredge both sides of the chicken in the flour, shaking off the excess.

In a large skillet over medium-high heat, warm the oil until a few droplets of water sizzle when carefully sprinkled in the pan. In two batches so as not to overcrowd the pan, cook the meat until nicely browned and cooked through, about 3 minutes per side. Transfer the meat to a plate and tent with foil to keep warm. Drain all of the fat from the pan.

For the sauce, add the stock and lemon juice to the pan and cook over medium-high heat, stirring with a wooden spoon to scrape up the browned bits from the bottom, until the sauce is reduced by half, about 3 minutes. Whisk in the butter. Stir in the sliced lemons and cook until warmed through, 1 to 2 minutes. Season with salt and pepper to taste.

To serve, place a piece of chicken on each plate and spoon the sauce over the top.

SERVES 4.

**V VARIATION:** *If you have capers in your pantry, you can add a spoonful to the sauce for a chicken piccata. The saltiness of the capers is a nice addition to the lemony sauce.*

**WEEKNIGHT CLASSIC**

# PA'S HERBED CHICKEN PARTS

*My kids love to eat chicken wings and drumettes—they call them "chicken parts." My dad (affectionately known as Pa by my girls) often makes this simple yet flavorful version for Sunday lunch. By cooking them slowly at a lower temperature, they almost start to caramelize, resulting in a delicious, crunchy skin.*

3 pounds chicken buffalo wingettes
1/2 cup olive oil
1 tablespoon dried rosemary
1 tablespoon dried thyme leaves

1 tablespoon dried oregano
Kosher salt and freshly ground black
    pepper

Preheat the oven to 350 degrees. Line a rimmed baking sheet with parchment paper.

Rinse the chicken and pat dry with paper towels. Place the chicken wings in a large bowl. Add the olive oil, rosemary, thyme, and oregano and toss to coat. Generously season with salt and pepper.

Place the chicken on the prepared baking sheet and evenly spread in a single layer. Bake, turning once, until golden and cooked through, about 1 hour. Serve warm.

SERVES 4.

Ⓥ **VARIATION:** *Instead of dried herbs, you can toss the chicken in a barbecue dry rub or Creole seasoning for a spicier end result.*

# PEANUT-Y FRIED CHICKEN STRIPS WITH MAPLE-DIJON DIPPING SAUCE

*The crunchy, nutty crust of these chicken tenders raises the bar! These are sure to become a family favorite.*

### MAPLE-DIJON DIPPING SAUCE

1/2 cup mayonnaise
2 tablespoons Dijon mustard
1/4 cup real maple syrup
Kosher salt and freshly ground black
　　pepper

### CHICKEN STRIPS

1 1/2 cups panko bread crumbs
1 1/2 cups cocktail peanuts
1/2 cup all-purpose flour
Kosher salt and freshly ground black
　　pepper
3 large eggs, lightly beaten
4 boneless, skinless chicken breasts
　　(about 1 1/2 pounds)
Vegetable oil, for frying

■ **TO PREPARE THE MAPLE-DIJON DIPPING SAUCE:** In a medium bowl whisk together the mayonnaise, mustard, and maple syrup. Season with salt and pepper to taste. Cover and refrigerate until ready to serve.

■ **TO PREPARE THE CHICKEN:** Preheat the oven to 350 degrees. Line a baking sheet with parchment paper.

■ Place the bread crumbs and peanuts in a food processor and process until finely ground. Place the mixture in a shallow bowl. Place the flour in another shallow bowl and season generously with salt and pepper. Place the beaten eggs in a third shallow bowl.

■ Rinse the chicken and pat dry with

paper towels. Slice each chicken breast lengthwise into 4 or 5 strips. Generously season the chicken with salt and pepper. Working in small batches, lightly dredge both sides of the chicken in the seasoned flour, shaking off the excess. Next dip the chicken in the egg wash to coat completely, letting the excess drip off. Then dredge the chicken through the peanut mixture, evenly coating on all sides. Place the prepared chicken on a baking sheet or cutting board.

■ In a large stockpot or Dutch oven pour enough oil so that there is approximately a 1-inch layer of oil. Over medium-high heat, warm the oil until a few droplets of water sizzle when carefully sprinkled in

the pot. In batches so as not to overcrowd the pot, cook the chicken until golden brown, about 3 minutes per side. Transfer the chicken to a baking sheet lined with parchment paper. Transfer to the oven and bake until the chicken is cooked through, 15 to 20 minutes. Serve warm with the dipping sauce on the side.

SERVES 4 TO 6.

**COOKING TIP:** *Mixed cocktail nuts can be substituted for the peanuts.*

**FREEZES WELL:** *The prepared but uncooked chicken fingers freeze well. To prevent sticking, freeze the chicken fingers in a single layer on a baking sheet before placing them in a container or freezer bag. When you are ready to cook the chicken fingers, no need to thaw. You can fry them frozen.*

# MIMI AND POP'S MARINATED GRILLED CHICKEN

*Wow! This is a deliciously simple way to dress up a piece of chicken. My friend Lee Schaffler learned this recipe from her grandparents, aka Mimi and Pop. To complete the meal, she recommends brushing some of that reserved marinade onto thinly sliced bread and grilling it until lightly toasted. I tried it and wholeheartedly agree!*

1/2 cup (1 stick) unsalted butter
5 cloves garlic, minced
1/4 cup cider vinegar
1/4 cup Worcestershire sauce
1/4 cup water
Juice and zest of 1 lemon
3 tablespoons orange juice

Dash of hot sauce
4 split, bone-in chicken breasts
   (about 3 pounds)
Vegetable oil, for the grates
Kosher salt and freshly ground black
   pepper

Place the butter, garlic, cider vinegar, Worcestershire, water, lemon juice, lemon zest, orange juice, and hot sauce in a medium saucepan. Bring the mixture to a boil over high heat. Reduce the heat to medium and simmer uncovered until the flavors have melded, about 10 minutes. Measure out 1/4 cup of marinade and reserve in the refrigerator while the chicken is marinating.

Rinse the chicken and pat dry with paper towels. Put the chicken in a nonreactive dish (glass or ceramic) just large enough to hold the chicken in a single layer, or use a resealable plastic bag. Pour the marinade over the chicken and toss to coat. Cover, place in the refrigerator, and marinate for at least 2 hours or overnight.

Preheat a clean grill to medium-high with the lid closed for 8 to 10 minutes. Lightly brush the grates with oil.

Remove the chicken from the marinade. Discard the used marinade. Generously season the chicken with salt and pepper.

Place the chicken on the grill. Close the lid and cook, turning once or twice, until no longer pink in the middle, 12 to 15 minutes per side. During the final 5 minutes of cooking, baste the chicken with the reserved marinade. Serve warm.

SERVES 4.

 **COOKING TIP:** *It may sound simple to an experienced cook, but I learned this the hard way when I first started cooking. You should always zest your lemon before juicing it. I like to use a plane zester and zest it straight into the bowl (or pot in this case) for less mess.*

# SLOW COOKER COLA CHICKEN

*I wish I could remember who originally gave me this recipe. It was so easy that I never forgot how to make it. Slow cooker dishes like this are ideal for busy weeknight meals. You just throw all the ingredients in a slow cooker in the morning, and come dinnertime, it's ready to go.*

4 split, bone-in, skin-on chicken breasts (about 3 pounds)
Kosher salt and freshly ground black pepper

1 yellow onion, peeled and quartered
1 lemon, quartered
1 (18-ounce) bottle barbecue sauce
1 (12-ounce) can cola (not diet)

Rinse the chicken and pat dry with paper towels. Generously season with salt and pepper. Place the chicken in a slow cooker. Add the onion and lemon. Pour the barbecue sauce and soda over the top.

Cover and cook on low for 6 to 8 hours or on high about 4 hours.

Serve warm with a ramekin of the cooking liquid on the side as a dipping sauce.

SERVES 4.

**COOKING TIPS:** *Slow cookers cook best when the lid remains tightly in place. Opening the lid often will require additional cooking time. Please refer to your machine's instructions.*

*You need at least a 3 ½-quart slow cooker for this recipe.*

**V VARIATION:** *You can use any cut of chicken in this foolproof recipe.*

**FREEZES WELL**

# MEAT

**MANY OF THE DISHES IN THIS CHAPTER ARE PERFECT FOR SUNDAY SUPPER.**
These are rich, meaty dishes that are simple to prepare but require time in the oven to become tender and delicious.

Sunday supper is a tradition in our family. It is the day we slow down our busy pace of life. The whole family (and often some friends who might as well be kin) gather around the table for a lazy and delicious meal.

Grillades (page 100) over grits has been a family favorite as long as I can remember. When I was a little girl, my grandmother would make it on holidays. The whole extended family (often twenty-plus of us) would gather at her house for a delicious dinner featuring this Louisiana specialty. Now my dad makes a big batch every time my sisters come into town to visit.

Dishes like Country Fried Steak with Onion Gravy (page 95) warm the soul and the belly on a cold winter day. I am so thankful to my friends the Sharps for sharing their family recipe with me. Served simply with a big bowl of white rice and some steamed broccoli, it's a meal my family loves.

I encourage you to make Sunday supper a tradition at your house. I guarantee it will become your favorite day of the week!

With all this talk of lazy meals, I must point out that not all meat dishes in this chapter require big chunks of time. My quick-cooking Pantry Pork Tenderloin (page 111) and Honey-Balsamic Flank Steak (page 102) are perfect for weeknight suppers. Keep Louisiana Meat Pies (page 106) in your freezer to throw in the oven on those days when you don't really have time to cook.

**COOKING TIP:** *Beef cubed steak is round steak that has been tenderized. If your local grocery does not have the tenderized steak displayed in the case, you can purchase round steak and ask the butcher to tenderize it for you.*

# COUNTRY FRIED STEAK WITH ONION GRAVY

*This is classic Southern food at its best! While many country fried steaks are tough, this version is super tender since it is slow-cooked in onion gravy. My friend Will Sharp's mother, Mary, deserves the credit for this recipe. When she was dating her husband, they used to enjoy this dish at a downtown Memphis restaurant once a week. As a surprise for her husband, she asked the cook for the recipe when she got married. She has been making it for her family ever since.*

2 pounds beef cubed steak (about 8 pieces)
Kosher salt and freshly ground black pepper
3/4 cup all-purpose flour, divided
Vegetable oil, for frying

1/4 cup (1/2 stick) unsalted butter
3 cups water
1 large yellow onion, thinly sliced

Preheat the oven to 300 degrees.

Generously season both sides of the steak with salt and pepper. Place 1/2 cup flour in a shallow bowl and lightly dredge both sides of the steak in the flour, shaking off the excess.

In a large stockpot or Dutch oven pour enough oil so that there is approximately a 1/4-inch layer of oil. Over medium-high heat, warm the oil until a few droplets of water sizzle when carefully sprinkled in the pot. In batches so as not to overcrowd the pot, cook the steak until browned, about 3 minutes per side. Transfer the steak to a baking sheet.

Drain all the fat from the pot. Add the butter to the same pan and heat over medium-low, stirring with a wooden spoon to scrape up the browned bits. When the butter starts to foam, add the remaining 1/4 cup flour and cook, whisking, until golden brown, 2 to 3 minutes. While continuing to whisk, gradually add the water. Simmer, whisking constantly, until the mixture just starts to come together as a sauce, about 3 minutes. (You do not want it to thicken too much as the sauce will continue to thicken as it cooks in the oven.) Season with salt and pepper to taste. Remove the pan from the heat. Return the steak and any juices to the pot. Spread the onions evenly over the steak.

Cover and bake until the meat is tender and cooked through, about 1 1/2 hours. Serve warm with gravy spooned over the meat.

**SERVES 6 TO 8.**

# FRIED PORK MEDALLIONS WITH WHITE MILK GRAVY

*Nick Vergos's Greek mother is the inspiration for a lot of his cooking. And while the traditional Greek specialties of spanakopita and souvlaki are still mainstays at her Sunday dinners, one of her specialties is Southern fried chicken and white milk gravy. To make this recipe a quick weekday supper, Nick decided to replace the whole fried chicken with cut-up pork medallions, pounded thin and quickly fried on the stovetop in a cast-iron skillet. Of course, you can always fry up a chicken and serve it with this yummy gravy!*

## PORK MEDALLIONS

1 cup all-purpose flour
$1/4$ teaspoon onion powder
1 pork tenderloin (about 1 $1/4$ pounds)
Kosher salt and freshly ground black
　　pepper
Vegetable oil, for frying

## WHITE MILK GRAVY

2 tablespoons unsalted butter
2 tablespoons all-purpose flour
2 cups 2% or whole milk
$1/8$ teaspoon cayenne pepper
Kosher salt and freshly ground black
　　pepper

Preheat the oven to 200 degrees.

TO PREPARE THE PORK: In a shallow bowl whisk together the flour and onion powder.

Rinse the pork and pat dry with paper towels. Cut the tenderloin into 1-inch thick slices. Place the slices in between 2 pieces of wax paper or plastic wrap, and using a meat mallet or rolling pin, pound to $1/8$ inch thick. Generously season both sides of the pork medallions with salt and pepper. Lightly dredge both sides of the pork in the seasoned flour, shaking off the excess.

In a large cast-iron skillet or Dutch oven, pour enough oil so that there is approximately a $1/2$-inch layer of oil. Over medium-high heat, warm the oil until a few droplets of water sizzle when carefully sprinkled in the pot. In batches so as not to overcrowd the pot, cook the pork until golden brown, 3 to 4 minutes per side. Transfer the pork to a rimmed baking sheet lined with a wire baking rack. Tent with foil and place in the oven to keep warm.

TO PREPARE THE GRAVY: Drain all of the fat from the pan.

Place the butter in the pan and melt over medium-low heat, stirring with a wooden spoon to scrape up the bits on the bottom. When the butter starts to foam, add the flour and cook, whisking,

until thickened, about 1 minute. While continuing to whisk, gradually add the milk. Increase the heat to medium-high and cook, whisking constantly, until the mixture comes to a boil, about 5 minutes.

As soon as it comes to a boil, remove from the heat and season with the cayenne pepper and salt and pepper to taste.

To serve, place a piece of pork on each plate and spoon the gravy over the top.

**SERVES 4.**

🥘 **COOKING TIP:** *Sorry to tell you this, but you can't make milk gravy with skim milk. You must use 2% or higher milk or the gravy will be too watery.*

# GRANDMA'S MEATLOAF

*If my grandma made meatloaf (which sadly she doesn't), this is what I imagine it would taste like: juicy and full of flavor with that iconic thin layer of ketchup on top. Whatever recipe you use, the trick to having a moist meatloaf is to add a little cheese in the mix.*

6 slices bacon
1/2 cup finely diced yellow onion (1 small onion)
1/2 cup thinly sliced celery (2 stalks)
1 clove garlic, minced
1/4 cup shredded carrots (1 carrot)
1 large egg
3 tablespoons 2% or whole milk
1 cup Italian-style bread crumbs

1 tablespoon Worcestershire sauce
1 tablespoon Dijon mustard
2 tablespoons tomato paste
2 pounds ground beef (80/20)
1/2 cup shredded mozzarella cheese
Kosher salt and freshly ground black pepper
1/4 cup ketchup

■ Preheat the oven to 350 degrees. Line a baking sheet with parchment paper or lightly spray with cooking spray.

■ In a large skillet over medium heat, cook the bacon until evenly browned and crispy. Remove with a slotted spoon and transfer to a plate lined with paper towels to drain. Crumble into small pieces once it has cooled enough to handle.

■ Drain all but 1 tablespoon of fat from the pan. Add the onion, celery, garlic, and carrots. Cook, stirring frequently, until the vegetables are soft, about 5 minutes. Set aside to cool to room temperature, about 5 minutes.

■ In a large bowl combine the egg, milk, bread crumbs, Worcestershire, mustard, and tomato paste. Stir until well combined. Add the beef, cooled vegetable mixture, cheese, and bacon. Season with salt and pepper to taste. Gently mix together by hand.

■ Form the meatloaf mixture into a log, about 6 inches long and 4 inches wide, and place it on the prepared baking sheet. Bake for 45 minutes. Remove from the oven and brush the top with the ketchup. Return to the oven and bake until the meatloaf is firm and cooked through, about 20 more minutes. Rest for 5 minutes before slicing. Serve warm.

**SERVES 6.**

**COOKING TIPS:** *The secret to a moist, tender meatloaf is to use a light touch when combining the ingredients. Overmixing compacts the meat, leading to dry, tough results.*

*If you want to make sure that the meatloaf is seasoned to your liking, cook a tablespoon-size patty in a skillet until cooked through. Taste and adjust seasonings as desired.*

**PANTRY SHORTCUT:** *Only have plain bread crumbs? Make them "Italian-style" by adding 2 teaspoons Italian herb seasoning to 1 cup of the plain bread crumbs.*

**DO-AHEAD:** *Meatloaf can be assembled and refrigerated one day in advance.*

**FREEZES WELL:** *Meatloaf freezes well before cooking. Make a double batch and freeze the extra loaf for another night. You can also freeze the meatloaf in individual servings if you prefer. Thaw before baking.*

# GRILLADES

*Grillades (pronounced "Gree-yades") are the Creole version of pot roast. Thin cuts of beef or veal are slow-cooked in a flavorful tomato sauce. In Louisiana, they are most often served over creamy grits. My family also serves them spooned over a bed of white rice.*

2 round steaks (about 1 pound each), thinly sliced
Kosher salt and freshly ground black pepper
2 tablespoons olive oil
1 cup diced yellow onion (1 large onion)
1 cup diced green bell pepper (1 large pepper)
1/4 cup thinly sliced celery (1 stalk)
1 tablespoon dried oregano

1 tablespoon dried thyme leaves
3 bay leaves
1 (28-ounce) can whole tomatoes
1 (6-ounce) can tomato paste
2 cups water
1 1/2 cups carrots cut on the bias about 1/2 inch thick (4 to 6 carrots)
6 cups Creamy Stone-Ground Grits (page 162) or cooked rice, warm

▨ Trim the fat off the meat and cut into 2-inch square medallions. Generously season the meat with salt and pepper.

▨ In a large stockpot or Dutch oven over medium-high heat, warm the oil until a few droplets of water sizzle when carefully sprinkled in the pot. In two batches so as to not crowd the pan, cook the meat, turning once, until nicely browned, about 10 minutes. Transfer the meat to a plate. Drain all but about 1 tablespoon of fat from the pot.

▨ To the pot add the onion, green pepper, celery, oregano, thyme, and bay leaves. Lower the temperature to medium-low and cook, stirring often, until very soft, about 10 minutes. Add the tomatoes, tomato paste, and water. Season with salt and pepper to taste. Return the meat to the pot and add the carrots. Bring the sauce to a boil over high heat, lower the heat to medium-low, and simmer, covered, until the meat is very tender, about 2 hours.

▨ Serve warm over grits or rice.

**SERVES 4 TO 6.**

**COOKING TIP:** *The technique of braising can turn the toughest cut of meat into a dish so tender you can cut it with a fork.*

**FREEZES WELL**

# HONEY-BALSAMIC FLANK STEAK

*This simple marinade is great for all types of steaks. It's full of flavor and uses ingredients I always have on hand.*

1/2 cup balsamic vinegar
1/4 cup honey
1 tablespoon Worcestershire sauce
3 cloves garlic, minced
1/4 teaspoon crushed red pepper flakes

1 flank steak (about 1 1/2 pounds)
Vegetable oil, for the grates
Kosher salt and freshly ground black
   pepper

In a shallow nonreactive dish (glass or ceramic) just large enough to hold the meat, stir together the balsamic vinegar, honey, Worcestershire, garlic, and red pepper flakes. Place the flank steak in the marinade and turn to coat. Marinate at room temperature for 20 to 30 minutes.

Preheat a clean grill to medium with the lid closed for 8 to 10 minutes. Lightly brush the grates with oil.

Remove the flank steak from the marinade, shaking off the excess liquid. Discard the marinade. Generously season the steak with salt and pepper.

Place the steak on the grill. Close the lid and cook, turning once, until desired temperature, 4 to 5 minutes per side for medium-rare or 5 to 6 minutes per side for medium. Remove the steak from the heat and set aside to rest for 5 minutes. Thinly slice across the grain before serving.

**SERVES 4.**

**COOKING TIPS:** *To make the honey easier to pour and to stir into the vinegar, I often heat it for 10 seconds in the microwave before adding it to the marinade.*

 *If you don't have a meat thermometer, you can use the "touch" test. As meat cooks, it gets firmer to the touch. Rare is really spongy and soft (like the flesh between your thumb and index finger when you pinch them together), medium is springy (like the flesh between your thumb and ring finger when you pinch them together), and well-done feels very firm.*

*Flank steak can be cooked indoors on a grill pan or broiled in the oven.*

### ⊞ WEEKNIGHT CLASSIC

# INDOOR SMOKY PORK BUTT

*My friend Chris Posey gave me this simple recipe for making a Boston pork butt so tender and smoky that no one would ever guess it was cooked indoors in the oven! He likes to serve the pork on yeast or sweet Hawaiian rolls with a little slaw on top.*

5 pounds pork butt, trimmed
1/2 cup prepared yellow mustard
1/2 cup barbecue dry rub seasoning

1/2 cup liquid steak marinade
2 tablespoons liquid smoke

Rinse the pork and pat dry with paper towels. Place the pork on a double layer of plastic wrap. Evenly slather all sides with the mustard. Generously season the pork butt with the dry rub. Tightly wrap it in the plastic wrap. Place in the refrigerator to marinate overnight.

Preheat the oven to 325 degrees.

Place a double layer of aluminum foil in a roasting pan. Unwrap the marinated pork butt and place on the foil. In a small bowl whisk together the marinade and liquid smoke. Pour the mixture over the top of the pork and then wrap it tightly in the foil. Place in the oven and cook until the meat is tender and has reached an internal temperature of 170 degrees, about 4 hours.

Transfer the cooked pork to a cutting board with a well. Place any remaining juices in a serving dish and reserve.

Remove and discard the fatty portions and any bones from the pork butt. Pull the pork apart and return it to the cooking liquid in the serving dish to keep it juicy. Serve warm.

**SERVES 8 TO 10.**

**COOKING TIPS:** *Liquid smoke is an all-natural ingredient that is created from smoke piped through a special condenser. It gives food cooked indoors that smoky flavor that comes from outdoor grilling or smoking.*

*If you get a bigger or smaller piece of pork, just cook it until it reaches 170 degrees and is tender, about 45 minutes per pound.*

>> **PANTRY SHORTCUT:** *When making this recipe, Chris uses Dale's Steak Seasoning (Reduced Sodium Blend). Like many liquid steak seasonings, this Southern pantry staple is made of soy sauce and other spices. If you can't find it at your local market, you can substitute plain soy sauce.*

**V** **VARIATION:** *This tender pulled pork would also be delicious tossed with your favorite barbecue sauce. Strain off the cooking liquid before adding the barbecue sauce.*

**❋ FREEZES WELL**

# LOUISIANA MEAT PIES

(PHOTO ON PAGE 92)

*The town of Natchitoches, Louisiana, may be renowned for their extravagant Christmas light displays, but when I think of this place, I think of their tasty meat pies. They are the perfect handheld treat for just about any occasion. Think empanadas with a Cajun flair!*

1 tablespoon olive oil
½ pound ground beef (80/20)
¼ cup finely diced yellow onion (½ small onion)
¼ cup finely diced green bell pepper (½ small pepper)
1 clove garlic, minced
1 tablespoon tomato paste
1 teaspoon Creole seasoning (see page 236 for a homemade recipe)

Kosher salt and freshly ground black pepper
1 tablespoon all-purpose flour
1 tablespoon water
2 (9-inch) unbaked piecrusts, homemade or store-bought
1 large egg beaten with 1 tablespoon of water

Preheat the oven to 400 degrees. Line a baking sheet with parchment paper.

In a large saucepan over medium-high heat, warm the oil until a few droplets of water sizzle when carefully sprinkled in the pan. Add the meat and cook, breaking up the beef with a wooden spoon, until the meat is browned and cooked through,

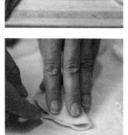

about 5 minutes. Transfer the cooked meat to a colander and drain off the excess fat.

▨ Drain all but about 1 tablespoon of fat from the pot. Add the onion, green pepper, and garlic. Reduce the heat to medium and cook, stirring occasionally, until soft, about 5 minutes. Return the meat to the pot and stir to combine. Stir in the tomato paste and Creole seasoning. Season with salt and pepper to taste. Cook until the flavors start to meld, about 3 minutes more. Adjust seasonings as needed. Dust the flour over the meat and add the water. Stir to combine. Transfer the mixture to a baking dish and place in the refrigerator to cool, about 15 minutes.

▨ Using a 4-inch round cookie cutter, cut the dough into 16 rounds. Lightly brush the outer edges of each circle with the egg wash.

▨ Place 1 heaping tablespoon of filling in the center of each round. Fold the circle over the filling to make a half-moon shape and pinch the edges together, making sure the pies are completely sealed. Using the back of a fork, crimp the edges. Transfer the pies to the prepared baking sheet and lightly brush the tops with the remaining egg wash. Bake until golden brown, about 25 minutes.

**SERVES 4.**

🍳 **COOKING TIP:** *To ensure perfectly shaped pies, it is important to let the filling cool before placing it on the dough. If the filling is hot, it will melt the dough. Also, the step I include of dusting the finished filling with flour and water helps bind the mixture so it won't leak moisture into the dough. These simple tricks can be used in any kind of savory or sweet handheld pie.*

❄️ **FREEZES WELL:** *Freeze assembled but uncooked pies on a baking sheet and then transfer them to a plastic freezer bag once frozen. To cook, thaw in the refrigerator and then bake following the directions above.*

# SAUSAGE AND PEPPERS OVER CHEESY GRITS

*Sausages are always a great solution for an easy yet super-flavorful supper. I always keep some Italian sausages in my freezer for sauces and quick-fix meals. I like to serve them over a bowlful of cheesy grits, but this recipe would also be delicious on a hoagie roll or over pasta.*

2 tablespoons olive oil
4 sweet Italian sausage links (about 1 pound)
1/2 cup thinly sliced green bell pepper
   (1 small pepper)
1/2 cup thinly sliced red bell pepper
   (1 small pepper)
1/2 cup thinly sliced yellow onion
   (1 small onion)

2 cloves garlic, minced
1 (15-ounce) can crushed tomatoes
1 teaspoon dried oregano
Kosher salt and freshly ground black
   pepper
6 cups Cheesy Instant Grits
   (see page 221 for the recipe), warm

In a large saucepan over medium-high heat, warm the oil until a few droplets of water sizzle when carefully sprinkled in the pan. Add the sausage links and cook until golden brown on all sides, about 5 minutes total. Transfer the links to a plate and reserve.

Pour all but 1 tablespoon of fat from the saucepan. Add the green peppers, red peppers, and onion and cook over medium heat until soft, about 5 minutes. Add the garlic and cook until fragrant, about 1 minute more. Add the tomatoes and oregano and stir to combine. Season with salt and pepper to taste. Add the sausage links back to the pan.

Bring the mixture to a boil over high heat. Reduce the heat to medium, cover, and simmer until the sausage links are cooked through, about 20 minutes.

To serve, portion the warm grits into serving bowls. Place a spoonful of sauce and a sausage link over the grits.

**SERVES 4.**

**Ⓥ VARIATION:** *If you want a spicier dish, you can use hot Italian sausage or add a teaspoon of crushed red pepper flakes to the sauce.*

**⊞ WEEKNIGHT CLASSIC**

# PANTRY PORK TENDERLOIN

*I came up with this simple marinade one day when I was going through my pantry trying to find a way to flavor a pork tenderloin when I was out of my usual marinade ingredients. I have to admit, it was so flavorful that this recipe is now my tried-and-true go-to! It goes to show, you can always find something tasty in a well-stocked kitchen pantry.*

1/2 cup plus 2 tablespoons olive oil, divided
2 tablespoons Dijon mustard
2 cloves garlic, minced
1/4 cup white wine vinegar
1 tablespoon dried rosemary
1 pork tenderloin (about 1 1/4 pounds), trimmed
Kosher salt and freshly ground black pepper

In a shallow nonreactive dish (glass or ceramic) just large enough to hold the meat in a single layer, stir together 1/2 cup olive oil, mustard, garlic, vinegar, and rosemary. Place the pork in the marinade and turn until well coated. Cover, place in the refrigerator, and marinate for at least 2 hours or overnight. Remove from the refrigerator 30 minutes before cooking.

Preheat the oven to 395 degrees.

Remove the pork from the marinade and shake off the excess. Discard the marinade. Season with salt and pepper to taste.

In a large cast-iron or ovenproof grill pan or skillet over medium-high heat, warm the remaining 2 tablespoons oil until a few droplets of water sizzle when carefully sprinkled in the pan. Sear the tenderloin until well browned on all sides, about 3 minutes per side. Transfer the tenderloin to the oven to finish cooking, 15 to 20 minutes.

Serve warm.

**SERVES 4.**

**COOKING TIPS:** *If you don't want to dirty a dish, you can always marinate your meat in a resealable plastic bag.*

*This recipe can also be made outdoors on the grill.*

# PAN-SEARED PORK CHOPS WITH DRUNKEN PEACHES

*Bourbon and peaches are two iconic Southern ingredients. Put them together and you have a tasty sauce for pork chops.*

4 bone-in, center-cut pork loin chops,
    each about 1 inch thick
Kosher salt and freshly ground black
    pepper
2 tablespoons olive oil
2 tablespoons unsalted butter

1/2 cup thinly sliced shallots (2 shallots)
1/2 teaspoon dried thyme leaves
1/4 cup bourbon
1 (16-ounce) bag frozen peaches, thawed
    and roughly chopped (about 2 cups)

▨ Preheat the oven to 395 degrees.

▨ Rinse the pork chops and pat them dry with paper towels. Generously season with salt and pepper. In a large cast-iron or ovenproof skillet over medium-high heat, warm the oil until a few droplets of water sizzle when carefully sprinkled in the skillet. Sear the chops until well browned on all sides, about 3 minutes per side. Place the chops in the oven to finish cooking, about 8 minutes for medium. Transfer the chops to a plate and cover with foil to keep warm.

▨ Pour all but 1 tablespoon of fat from the skillet. Add the butter and heat until foamy. Then add the shallots and thyme. Cook, stirring occasionally, over medium heat until soft, about 3 minutes. Add the bourbon and simmer uncovered until the liquor has almost evaporated, about 2 minutes. Add the peaches and cook until they are tender, about 3 minutes. Season with salt and pepper to taste.

▨ To serve, place a spoonful of the peach mixture over each chop.

**SERVES 4.**

🖐 **COOKING TIP:** *If you are unsure whether the pork (or any other meat) is fully cooked, use a meat thermometer. Pork is safe to eat when it is cooked to an internal temperature of 155 to 160 degrees.*

 WEEKNIGHT CLASSIC

# TAMALE PIE

*Tamale Pie is one of my favorite things to order from my friend Bradford Williams's prepared foods shop, Curbside Casserole. She was kind enough to share her recipe with me. In her shop, she makes it with house-smoked pulled pork, but for everyday convenience, I make it with ground beef.*

**FILLING**
1 tablespoon olive oil
1 pound ground beef (80/20)
1/2 cup diced yellow onion (1 small onion)
1/2 cup green bell pepper
  (1 small pepper)
2 cloves garlic, minced
1 (4-ounce) can chopped green chilies
1 (14-ounce) can diced tomatoes, drained
2 cups corn kernels, thawed if using frozen
1 tablespoon chili powder
1 tablespoon cumin

1/4 teaspoon cayenne pepper
Kosher salt and freshly ground pepper

**TOPPING**
4 cups water
1 teaspoon kosher salt, plus more for
  seasoning
1 cup quick-cooking grits
3 cups shredded sharp Cheddar cheese
2 cloves garlic, minced
Freshly ground pepper

Preheat the oven to 375 degrees.

TO PREPARE THE FILLING: In a large saucepan over medium-high heat, warm the oil until a few droplets of water sizzle when carefully sprinkled in the pan. Add the meat and cook, breaking up the beef with a wooden spoon, until the meat is browned and cooked through, about 5 minutes. Transfer the cooked meat to a colander and drain off the excess fat.

Drain all but about 1 tablespoon of fat from the pot. Add the onion and green pepper, reduce the heat to medium, and cook, stirring occasionally, until soft, about 5 minutes. Add the garlic and cook until fragrant, about 1 minute. Stir in the green chilies, tomatoes, corn, chili powder, cumin, and cayenne. Cook until warmed through, about 3 minutes. Return the meat to the pot and stir to combine. Season with salt and pepper to taste. Spoon the mixture into a 9 x 13-inch baking dish.

▪ **TO PREPARE THE TOPPING:** In a large saucepan over medium-high heat, bring the water and 1 teaspoon salt to a boil. Whisk in the grits. Reduce the heat to low, cover, and cook, whisking occasionally, until the liquid is absorbed, about 10 minutes. Stir in the cheese and the garlic and stir until well combined and the cheese has melted. Season with salt and pepper to taste.

▪ Spoon the grits over the top of the meat mixture in an even layer. Bake until golden brown, about 45 minutes. Serve warm.

**SERVES 6 TO 8.**

🖐 **COOKING TIP:** *To make your prep time more efficient, cook the grits at the same time you cook the meat filling.*

Ⓥ **VARIATION:** *If you want to make this with pulled pork, see my recipe for Indoor Smoky Pork Butt on page 104.*

# TAMALE PIE VARIATIONS

In place of the ground beef, try making your tamale pie with one of the following:

> 1 pound cooked pulled pork
> 1 pound cooked ground turkey
> 1 pound cooked shredded chicken
> 2 cans black beans

Just add your chosen protein to the filling at the same time you would normally stir in the cooked ground beef.

# FISH AND SHELLFISH

WHEN YOU WANT DINNER ON THE TABLE QUICKLY, FISH IS THE IDEAL choice because it cooks so fast. In this chapter, I specifically feature recipes that call for boneless fillets that can be quickly cooked for a weeknight meal.

When buying fish, the first rule of thumb is to buy what is freshest. Don't be shy. Ask to smell it. The fish should smell more like the ocean than dead fish. If it smells overly fishy, that means it is past its prime and will taste overly fishy too. Also, I have the fishmonger cut larger pieces of fish (like a side of salmon) into individual portions for me so I don't have to mess with cutting it at home. Keep that in mind when making dishes like Pan-Roasted Salmon with Field Pea Relish (page 128) or Showstopper Salmon (page 134).

Luckily for us, there is an incredibly wide variety of frozen fish and seafood now available at the grocery. And I am not talking about frozen breaded fish sticks! High-quality options like salmon, red snapper, and tilapia are now available for purchase. Shrimp come in several sizes and with the option of peeled and deveined for convenience. Keep a good variety in your freezer to save you a trip to the fish counter.

I also want to point out that although I call for specific types of fish in these recipes, use the variety you can find that is the freshest and the best quality. For example, the Trout Amandine (page 137) is just as delicious when made using sole or tilapia in place of the trout.

# BLACKENED RED SNAPPER

*Blackened fish is a Cajun way of preparing fish. It is a very simple technique as the blackening comes from a spicy dry rub that is put on the fish. All types of fish—including snapper, catfish, tilapia, grouper, salmon, and swordfish—taste delicious blackened. Try it with your favorite!*

4 red snapper fillets (6 ounces each)
4 tablespoons blackened seasoning (see
    page 235 for a homemade recipe)

2 tablespoons olive oil
Lemon wedges, for serving

 Season both sides of the fish with the blackened seasoning. In a large skillet over medium-high heat, warm the oil until a few droplets of water sizzle when carefully sprinkled in the pan. Sear the fish on one side until the meat is well browned and releases easily from the pan, 4 to 5 minutes. Turn over the fillets and cook until desired doneness, about 5 more minutes. Serve warm with lemon wedges.

**SERVES 4.**

⊞ **WEEKNIGHT CLASSIC**

# CATFISH BITES
# WITH KICKED-UP REMOULADE

*We are all about finger food in our house, and this is our favorite way to enjoy every Southerner's favorite fried fish.*

**REMOULADE DIPPING SAUCE**

3/4 cup mayonnaise

4 tablespoons ketchup

1 tablespoon Creole or whole grain
mustard

3 tablespoons freshly squeezed lemon
juice

Kosher salt and freshly ground black
pepper

**CATFISH**

2 cups buttermilk

1 tablespoon hot sauce

3 catfish fillets (about 6 ounces each),
cut into 1-inch pieces

1/3 cup all-purpose flour

Kosher salt and freshly ground black
pepper

2 large eggs, lightly beaten

1 cup yellow cornmeal

1 tablespoon sugar

1 teaspoon cayenne pepper

Vegetable oil, for frying

TO PREPARE THE REMOULADE SAUCE: In a medium bowl whisk together the mayonnaise, ketchup, mustard, and lemon juice. Season with salt and pepper to taste. Cover and refrigerate until ready to serve.

TO PREPARE THE CATFISH: In a large glass bowl, whisk together the buttermilk and hot sauce. Add the fish, toss to coat, and marinate at room temperature for 30 minutes.

Place the flour in a shallow bowl and generously season with salt and pepper. Place the beaten egg in another shallow bowl. Place the cornmeal, sugar, and cayenne in a third shallow bowl and whisk to combine.

Remove the fish from the milk in batches and shake the excess milk off the fish. Working in small batches, lightly dredge the fish in the seasoned flour, shaking off the excess. Next dip the fish in the egg wash to coat completely, letting the excess drip off. Then dredge the fish through the cornmeal mixture, evenly coating on all sides. Place the prepared fish on a baking sheet or cutting board.

In a large stockpot or Dutch oven pour enough oil so that there is approximately a 2-inch layer of oil. Over medium-high

heat, warm the oil until a few droplets of water sizzle when carefully sprinkled in the pot. In batches so as not to overcrowd the pot, cook the fish, turning to cook on all sides, until golden brown and cooked through, about 5 minutes. Transfer to a plate lined with paper towels to drain. Serve warm with the remoulade sauce.

**SERVES 4.**

👍 **COOKING TIP:** *On busy weeknights I try to be as efficient as possible. For recipes like this, I would suggest making the sauce and prepping the fry oil while the fish is marinating.*

✅ **DO-AHEAD:** *The remoulade dipping sauce can be made up to three days in advance. Cover and refrigerate until just before serving.*

# HORSERADISH ENCRUSTED GROUPER WITH LEMON BUTTER SAUCE

*Doesn't it just break your heart when one of your favorite restaurants closes? Jarrett's was one of my favorite places to eat in Memphis because of its great food and the gracious hospitality of its owners, Rick and Barbara Farmer. As anyone who dined there will tell you, Rick's Horseradish Encrusted Grouper was one of the most popular items in town. When Rick shared the recipe, I was shocked at how simple it was to prepare. So from his kitchen to yours . . . enjoy!*

### FISH
1/4 cup prepared horseradish
2 large eggs
1 cup panko bread crumbs
4 boneless grouper fillets
    (4 to 6 ounces each)
Kosher salt and freshly ground black pepper
2 tablespoons olive oil

### LEMON BUTTER SAUCE
6 tablespoons unsalted butter, melted
    and warm
1 tablespoon finely grated lemon zest
1 tablespoon freshly squeezed lemon
    juice
Kosher salt and freshly ground black
    pepper

▓ Preheat the oven to 375 degrees.

▓ **TO PREPARE THE FISH:** Place the horseradish and eggs in a shallow bowl and whisk to combine. Place the bread crumbs in another shallow bowl.

▓ Generously season the fish with salt and pepper. Dip the fish in the egg mixture to coat completely, letting the excess drip off. Then dredge the fish through the bread crumbs, evenly coating on all sides. Place the prepared fish on a baking sheet or cutting board.

▓ In a large ovenproof skillet over medium-high heat, warm the oil until a few droplets of water sizzle when carefully sprinkled in the pan. Sear the fish on one side until golden brown, 2 to 3 minutes. Turn over the fillets and cook until the other side is golden, about 2 minutes more. Transfer the fish to the oven and cook until desired doneness, about 6 more minutes for medium.

**TO PREPARE THE LEMON BUTTER SAUCE:** In a small bowl stir together the melted butter, lemon zest, and lemon juice. Season with salt and pepper to taste.

To serve, spoon the sauce onto each plate and place the fish on top. Serve immediately.

**SERVES 4.**

**COOKING TIP:** *For an extra horseradishy flavor, Rick recommends draining the prepared horseradish in a fine sieve before mixing with the eggs.*

**WEEKNIGHT CLASSIC**

# NEW ORLEANS BARBECUED SHRIMP

*I have always thought it funny that New Orleans barbecued shrimp has no barbecue sauce in it! Instead, the shrimp is cooked in a tasty garlic butter sauce flavored with Worcestershire and black pepper. This recipe is from my cousin Laura Burns, who is lucky to live on the Gulf Coast, where fresh shrimp is plentiful. Whether using fresh or frozen shrimp, be warned! This is one of those messy dishes that can only be eaten with your hands and with crusty French bread on the side to sop up that finger-lickin'-good sauce.*

1/2 cup (1 stick) unsalted butter
1/2 cup olive oil
1/3 cup Worcestershire sauce
2 tablespoons freshly ground black
    pepper
1 lemon, thinly sliced

1/4 teaspoon hot sauce
2 cloves garlic, minced
1/4 teaspoon paprika
1 teaspoon kosher salt
2 pounds unpeeled large shrimp
    (16/20 count), thawed if using frozen

Preheat the oven to 450 degrees.

Place the butter and olive oil in a medium saucepan. Over medium heat, warm until the butter is melted. Add the Worcestershire, black pepper, lemon slices, hot sauce, garlic, paprika, and salt. Stir to combine and simmer until the flavors meld together, 5 to 7 minutes.

Place the shrimp in a 9 x 13-inch baking pan. Pour the sauce over the top and toss to coat. Place in the oven and cook until the shrimp turn pink and are cooked through, 8 to 10 minutes. Serve warm.

**SERVES 4 TO 6.**

**COOKING TIP:** *Be careful not to overcook the shrimp or they will be chewy. Shrimp are done when they turn pink.*

**V VARIATION:** *This is a family-friendly version of barbecued shrimp. For a spicier version, add more black pepper, Worcestershire, and hot sauce to taste.*

**WEEKNIGHT CLASSIC**

# OVEN-FRIED TILAPIA

*Crispy fried fish is a staple in the South. But let's all be honest; sometimes on busy weeknights we want to have the crispy-crusted fish without having to deal with the mess of frying. I have found that panko bread crumbs seasoned with a little Southern spice can give a piece of baked fish a crispy coating that makes all of the fried fish lovers at my dinner table happy.*

1 1/2 cups panko bread crumbs
1/2 cup grated Parmesan cheese
1 teaspoon paprika
1 teaspoon Creole seasoning (see page 236 for a homemade recipe)

1/2 cup mayonnaise
4 tilapia fillets (4 to 6 ounces each)
Kosher salt and freshly ground black pepper
Lemon wedges, optional garnish

▦ Preheat the oven to 400 degrees. Line a rimmed baking sheet with parchment paper.

▦ Place the bread crumbs, Parmesan, paprika, and Creole seasoning in a shallow bowl and whisk to combine.

▦ Brush the mayonnaise on both sides of the fish. Generously season with salt and pepper. Dredge the fish through the bread crumb mixture, evenly coating on all sides. Place the fish on the prepared baking sheet.

▦ Bake until golden brown and cooked through, about 20 minutes. Serve warm with lemon wedges on the side if desired.

**SERVES 4.**

Ⓥ **VARIATION:** *This recipe would work well with other white fish like catfish and grouper.*

▦ **WEEKNIGHT CLASSIC**

# PAN-ROASTED SALMON WITH FIELD PEA RELISH

*Pan-roasting is the ideal way to cook fish. Sear the fish until it has a nice golden crust, and then finish cooking it in the oven to keep the fish moist and flaky. I use this same technique with all types of fish.*

**FIELD PEA RELISH**
1 (15-ounce) can black-eyed peas, rinsed and drained
2 tablespoons finely diced green bell pepper
2 tablespoons finely diced red onion
2 tablespoons finely diced pimentos or roasted red peppers
1 clove garlic, minced
2 tablespoons red wine vinegar

1 tablespoon olive oil
Kosher salt and freshly ground black pepper

**PAN-ROASTED SALMON**
4 salmon fillets (4 to 6 ounces each)
Kosher salt and freshly ground black pepper
2 tablespoons olive oil

▓ TO PREPARE THE FIELD PEA RELISH: In a medium bowl toss together the black-eyed peas, green pepper, red onion, pimentos, garlic, vinegar, and olive oil. Season with salt and pepper to taste. Cover and refrigerate until ready to serve.

▓ TO PREPARE THE FISH: Preheat the oven to 375 degrees.

▓ Generously season the salmon with salt and pepper. In a large ovenproof skillet over medium heat, warm the oil until a few water droplets sizzle when carefully sprinkled in the skillet. Sear the salmon, skin side up, until the meat is well browned and easily releases from pan, about 4 minutes. Flip over and cook until seared, about 1 minute. Transfer the pan to the oven and roast until the fish is medium-rare, about 5 minutes, or until desired doneness.

▓ Serve warm with a spoonful of relish on top.

**SERVES 4.**

🄴 **COOKING TIP:** *Jarred pimientos and roasted red peppers can be substituted for one another.*

**V VARIATION:** *In the summertime I use fresh lady peas from my local farmers' market in this recipe. To substitute fresh field peas for the canned, just boil the peas until tender, about 8 minutes, before tossing with the other ingredients.*

**✓ DO-AHEAD:** *The relish can be made up to one day in advance. Cover and refrigerate until ready to serve.*

**▦ WEEKNIGHT CLASSIC**

# SHRIMP CREOLE

*This iconic Louisiana dish is so popular not only because it's delicious but also because it is so easy to prepare. Since it can be made in just about thirty minutes, it is the perfect weeknight supper.*

1 1/2 pounds large shrimp (16/20 count), peeled and deveined, thawed if using frozen
1/2 teaspoon cayenne pepper
1/2 teaspoon paprika
3 tablespoons olive oil, divided
1/2 cup finely diced yellow onion (1 small onion)
1/2 cup finely diced green bell pepper (1 small pepper)
1/4 cup thinly sliced celery (1 stalk)
2 cloves garlic, minced
1 (28-ounce) can whole tomatoes with juice
1 tablespoon tomato paste
1/2 cup chicken stock or water
Kosher salt and freshly ground black pepper
6 cups cooked white rice, warm

Place the shrimp in a large bowl and toss with the cayenne pepper and paprika.

In a large saucepan over medium-high heat, warm 2 tablespoons of the oil until a few droplets of water sizzle when carefully sprinkled in the pan. Add the shrimp and cook, stirring occasionally, until the shrimp are lightly browned, 3 to 4 minutes. Transfer the cooked shrimp to a plate and reserve.

In the same pan over medium-high heat, warm the remaining 1 tablespoon oil until a few droplets of water sizzle when carefully sprinkled in the pan. Add the onion, green pepper, and celery, and cook, stirring occasionally, until soft, about 5 minutes. Add the garlic and cook until fragrant, about 1 minute more. Add the whole tomatoes and their juices, breaking them up with a spoon or fork. Add the tomato paste and stock. Stir to combine. Season with salt and pepper to taste. Bring the mixture to a boil over high heat. Reduce the heat to medium-low and simmer uncovered, stirring occasionally, until the sauce thickens, 20 to 25 minutes.

Return the shrimp to the pan and stir to combine. Cook until the shrimp are warmed through, 2 to 3 more minutes. Adjust seasonings as needed. Serve warm over white rice.

**SERVES 6.**

 🖐 **COOKING TIP:** *I find that canned whole tomatoes melt into a sauce better than canned diced tomatoes. To break them up, I like to cut them with my kitchen scissors while they are still in the can before adding them to the pot.*

🗓 **WEEKNIGHT CLASSIC**

# SNAPPER WITH MUSTARD-PECAN CRUST

*This mustard-nut crust turns a simple baked fish into a rich and elegant meal. I use pecans because that's the nut that I always have on hand, but this would also be delicious with hazelnuts or walnuts.*

**3 tablespoons unsalted butter, softened**
**1/4 cup Dijon mustard**
**1/2 cup finely chopped pecans**

**4 red snapper fillets (6 ounces each)**
**Kosher salt and freshly ground black**
**   pepper**

Line a rimmed baking sheet with parchment paper.

In a small bowl stir together the butter and mustard until creamy. Stir in the pecans until well combined. Generously season the fish with salt and pepper. Spread the butter mixture over the top of each of the fillets. Place on the prepared baking sheet and refrigerate for 30 minutes.

Preheat the oven to 500 degrees.

Transfer the fish to the oven and bake until the crust is golden and the fish is cooked through, 6 to 8 minutes. Serve warm.

**SERVES 4.**

**COOKING TIPS:** *Refrigerating the fish once you have added the crust mixture on top helps ensure that the crust stays on while cooking. Otherwise, it might melt too quickly and slide off the fish.*

*It is also very important to have the butter softened to room temperature in order to be able to cream it together with the Dijon mustard.*

**WEEKNIGHT CLASSIC**

# SHOWSTOPPER SALMON

*A few ingredients from your pantry can turn an everyday piece of salmon into a showstopper.*

2 tablespoons canola or vegetable oil
3 tablespoons soy sauce
3 tablespoons balsamic vinegar
2 tablespoons orange juice
2 tablespoons honey

3 cloves garlic, minced
1 tablespoon crushed red pepper flakes
1/2 teaspoon onion powder
4 salmon fillets (4 to 6 ounces each)
Vegetable oil, for the grates

In a small bowl whisk together the oil, soy sauce, balsamic vinegar, orange juice, honey, garlic, red pepper flakes, and onion powder. Measure out 2 tablespoons of the marinade and refrigerate until you grill the fish.

Put the salmon in a nonreactive dish (glass or ceramic) just large enough to hold the fish in a single layer. Pour the marinade over the fish and toss to coat. Cover and place in the refrigerator. Marinate for at least 30 minutes but no more than 1 hour.

Preheat a clean grill to medium-high with the lid closed for 8 to 10 minutes. Lightly brush the grates with oil.

Remove the salmon from the marinade. Discard the used marinade.

Place the salmon on the grill, flesh side down. Close the lid and cook for 3 to 4 minutes. Turn the salmon over and brush with the reserved marinade. Cook for 3 to 5 more minutes for medium. Serve warm.

**SERVES 4.**

**COOKING TIP:** *The secret to grilling salmon (or any fish) is to let a good crust form on the outside before you try to flip it. If you try to flip it before it is ready, the flesh will tear and fall apart.*

**WEEKNIGHT CLASSIC**

# TROUT AMANDINE

*When I think of trout amandine, I think of my Grandmother Hanemann. When I was a little girl and visited her in New Orleans, we would get all dressed up and she would take me out to eat trout amandine at her favorite restaurant. I wish I knew the name of the restaurant so I could take my girls there when we visit New Orleans, but at least I can treat them to this delicious dish at home with this surprisingly easy recipe.*

½ cup 2% or whole milk
½ cup all-purpose flour
4 trout fillets (5 to 6 ounces each)
Kosher salt and freshly ground black pepper

½ cup (1 stick) unsalted butter, divided
½ cup sliced almonds
Juice of 1 lemon

Place the milk in a shallow bowl and the flour in another shallow bowl. Generously season the fish with salt and pepper. Dip the fish in the milk, shaking off the excess. Then lightly dredge both sides of the fish in the flour, shaking off the excess. Place the prepared fish on a baking sheet or cutting board.

In a large skillet over medium-high heat, melt 4 tablespoons of the butter. In two batches so as not to overcrowd the pan, cook the fish until golden brown on both sides and cooked through, about 3 minutes per side. Transfer the fish to a plate and tent with foil to keep warm.

Add the remaining 4 tablespoons butter to the pan and cook over medium-high heat, stirring with a wooden spoon to scrape up the browned bits from the bottom, until the butter stops foaming and begins to brown, about 3 minutes. Reduce the heat to low, stir in the almonds, and cook until warmed through, 1 to 2 minutes. Add the lemon juice and season with salt and pepper to taste.

To serve, place a piece of fish on each plate and spoon the sauce over the top.

**SERVES 4.**

**COOKING TIP:** *This recipe works well with any light flaky fish. I have made it with tilapia and sole when my market was out of trout.*

**WEEKNIGHT CLASSIC**

# PASTA AND RICE MAINS

GOT A BOX OF RICE OR PASTA IN THE PANTRY? THEN YOU HAVE SUPPER! These two ingredients make a quick, easy, and economical base for a multitude of Southern dishes. Grown in several Southern states (including Arkansas, Louisiana, and South Carolina), rice is an essential ingredient in the South.

Since my family is from Louisiana, I grew up with rice, not potatoes, as our everyday starchy side. Rice-based dishes like Jambalaya (page 140) and Weeknight Red Beans and Rice (page 153) were some of my favorites. In fact, my Uncle Buddie made them best . . . Sorry, Dad! Being a die-hard Creole cook, my uncle may not approve of the Weeknight Red Beans and Rice I share in this book, but some days I want a steamy bowlful of this favorite without the fuss of soaking dry beans.

Creamy pasta dishes like Chicken Spaghetti (page 144) and Creamy Mac 'n' Cheese (page 146) are always crowd pleasers for the kids at the table. And if you pay attention, the grown-ups at your table will be enjoying these comfort dishes just as much . . . if not more!

# ANDOUILLE JAMBALAYA

*This iconic Louisiana dish has many variations. Some folks use chicken, others add shrimp, and, as I do in this recipe, some use just pork. Having been born in Louisiana, I am a purist when it comes to which kind of pork sausage to use: hands down, it has to be Andouille. This smoked Cajun sausage used to be hard to find outside the state of Louisiana, but now most groceries carry it. I always keep a pound or two in my freezer since it is used in so many classic Cajun dishes.*

½ pound bacon (about 10 slices), cut into ½-inch pieces
1 pound Andouille smoked sausage, thinly sliced into rounds
½ cup finely diced yellow onion (1 small onion)
½ cup seeded and finely diced green bell pepper (1 small pepper)
¼ cup finely diced celery (1 stalk)

2 cloves garlic, minced
1 teaspoon dried oregano
1 teaspoon dried thyme leaves
2 bay leaves
Kosher salt and freshly ground black pepper
1 (15-ounce) can tomato sauce
4 cups chicken stock
3 cups uncooked white rice

In a large stockpot or Dutch oven over medium-high heat, cook the bacon until lightly browned and the fat is rendered, about 3 minutes. Remove with a slotted spoon and transfer to a plate lined with paper towels to drain. In the same pot, cook the sausage until browned on all sides, about 5 minutes. Transfer the sausage to the plate with the bacon. Drain all but about 1 tablespoon of fat from the pot.

Add the onion, green pepper, and celery, and cook, stirring often, until soft, about 5 minutes. Add the garlic, oregano, thyme, and bay leaves, and cook until the mixture is cooked down, about 5 minutes more. Season with salt and pepper to taste.

While the vegetable mixture is cooking, combine the tomato sauce and chicken stock in a separate pot. Bring to a simmer over medium-high heat.

Add the rice to the vegetable mixture and cook, stirring, until translucent, about 3 minutes. Return the meats to the pot and stir to combine. Slowly pour the hot tomato and stock mixture into the jambalaya, stirring to combine evenly.

Bring the jambalaya to a boil over high heat. Reduce the heat to medium-low, cover, and simmer until the rice is tender and most of the liquid has been absorbed, about 30 minutes. Serve warm.

**SERVES 6 TO 8.**

**V VARIATION:** *Andouille sausage is a smoked, spicy pork sausage that is popular in Cajun recipes such as gumbo and jambalaya. If you can't easily find it in your local grocery, any smoked sausage is an acceptable substitute.*

# CAJUN CHICKEN ALFREDO

*A decadently creamy Alfredo sauce is probably the quickest and easiest pasta sauce to whip up. Serve it plain over your favorite pasta, or give it a spicy Cajun kick like I do in this version.*

4 boneless, skinless chicken breasts (about 1 1/2 pounds)
2 tablespoons blackened seasoning (see page 235 for a homemade recipe)
2 tablespoons olive oil
1 cup heavy cream

2 tablespoons unsalted butter
1 cup freshly grated Parmesan cheese
Kosher salt and freshly ground black pepper
1 (16-ounce) box fettuccine, cooked per package directions and kept warm
1 cup cherry tomatoes, halved

Preheat the oven to 375 degrees.

Rinse the chicken and pat dry with paper towels. Season both sides of the chicken with the blackened seasoning.

In a large cast-iron or ovenproof skillet over medium-high heat, warm the oil until a few droplets of water sizzle when carefully sprinkled in the pan. Cook the chicken until nicely browned on both sides, 2 to 3 minutes per side. Place the chicken in the oven and cook until done, about 8 more minutes. Place the chicken on a cutting board and let rest for 5 minutes. Thinly slice against the grain and tent with foil to keep warm.

In a medium saucepan over medium-high heat, bring the heavy cream and butter to a boil. Reduce the heat to medium-low. Stir in the Parmesan and cook until melted. Remove the sauce from the heat. Season with salt and pepper to taste.

In a large bowl toss together the warm pasta, sauce, chicken, and tomatoes. Season with salt and pepper to taste. Serve immediately.

**SERVES 6 TO 8.**

**V** VARIATION: *This dish would also be delicious with blackened shrimp.*

**⊞** WEEKNIGHT CLASSIC

# CHICKEN SPAGHETTI

*This should really be called Chicken Tommy. In the Prest household, the boys have renamed this classic spaghetti casserole after each other based on which veggies are added. Our dear friend Tommy likes his with carrots and peas. His brother's version, Chicken Christopher, has no peas. I think it would also be good with sautéed mushrooms. Basically, it's one of those dishes you can easily customize to suit your own taste!*

8 ounces dry spaghetti, broken into 2-inch pieces
1/2 cup peeled and finely sliced carrots (2 carrots)
1/2 cup frozen peas, thawed
4 tablespoons unsalted butter
1/4 cup finely diced yellow onion (1/2 small onion)
4 tablespoons all-purpose flour
1 cup 2% or whole milk
2 cups chicken stock, divided
3 cups shredded sharp Cheddar cheese, divided
1/4 cup mayonnaise
1/8 teaspoon cayenne
Kosher salt and freshly ground black pepper
2 cups shredded cooked chicken

Preheat the oven to 350 degrees.

Cook the spaghetti according to package directions. Drain and set aside.

Fill a small saucepan with water and bring to a boil over high heat. Add the carrots and peas and cook until crisp-tender, about 8 minutes. Drain well and set aside.

In a large saucepan over medium heat, melt the butter. Add the onions and cook until soft, about 5 minutes. Add the flour and cook, whisking, until golden brown, 2 to 3 minutes.

While continuing to whisk, gradually add the milk and 1 cup of the chicken stock. Bring the mixture to a boil over medium-high heat. Reduce the heat to medium-low and simmer, whisking constantly, until the mixture thickens to the consistency of canned soup, 5 to 8 minutes. Stir in the remaining cup of chicken stock. Add 2 cups of the cheese and stir until melted. Remove the pan from the heat. Stir in the mayonnaise and cayenne. Season with salt and pepper to taste.

Add the cooked spaghetti, peas, carrots, and chicken, and stir to combine. Adjust the seasonings as necessary. Pour the filling into a 9 x 13-inch baking dish.

Sprinkle the remaining 1 cup of cheese evenly over the top.

Bake until golden brown and bubbling, about 45 minutes.

**SERVES 6 TO 8.**

» **PANTRY SHORTCUT:** *Two cans of cream of chicken soup can be substituted for the homemade cream sauce. Just warm the soup over medium heat and whisk in 1 cup chicken stock, 2 cups of cheese, and mayonnaise. Season and stir in the remaining ingredients.*

❄ FREEZES WELL

# CREAMY MAC 'N' CHEESE

*You will be surprised at how easy it is to whip up a homemade mac 'n' cheese. No need to reach for the boxed variety again once you have this creamy and cheesy recipe in your repertoire.*

4 tablespoons unsalted butter
2 tablespoons all-purpose flour
1 1/2 cups 2% or whole milk
1 cup shredded sharp Cheddar cheese

Kosher salt and freshly ground black pepper
8 ounces macaroni, cooked per package directions

In a medium saucepan over medium-low heat, melt the butter. When the butter starts to foam, add the flour and cook, whisking, until thickened, about 1 minute. While continuing to whisk, gradually add the milk. Bring the mixture to a boil over medium-high heat. Reduce the heat to medium-low and simmer, whisking constantly, until the mixture thickens, 5 to 8 minutes. Remove the pan from the heat.

Stir in the cheese until melted. Season with salt and pepper to taste. Pour the macaroni into the cheese sauce and stir until well coated. If the sauce is too thick, add some extra milk, 1 tablespoon at a time, until the desired consistency. Serve warm.

**SERVES 4.**

**V VARIATIONS:** *Other cheeses like Gruyere and white Cheddar would also make a delicious cheesy sauce for this dish. Experiment with your favorites and what you have on hand.*

**WEEKNIGHT CLASSIC**

**COOKING TIP:** *Add your favorite hot sauce for a little heat.*

**VARIATIONS:** *Variations for this recipe abound, most concerning the type of pork used. I use bacon because that's what I keep in my pantry. The more traditional ham hock can be substituted for the bacon if you prefer. For a vegetarian version, just omit the pork altogether.*

**DO-AHEAD:** *Cooked peas store very well in the refrigerator. Some even say they taste better the second day.*

# HOPPIN' JOHN

*Hoppin' John is a classic Southern dish that is most famous for its place at the dinner table on the first day of the year. Simple yet hearty fare, Hoppin' John is a flavorful mixture of black-eyed peas, rice, smoked pork, and onions.*

1 pound dried black-eyed peas, rinsed and sorted
1 tablespoon olive oil
1/2 cup finely diced yellow onion (1 small onion)
1/2 cup finely diced green bell pepper (1 small pepper)
1/4 cup finely sliced celery (1 stalk)
2 cloves garlic, minced
1 teaspoon dried oregano
1 teaspoon dried thyme

1 teaspoon Creole seasoning (see page 236 for a homemade recipe)
2 bay leaves
Kosher salt and freshly ground black pepper
1/4 pound bacon, cut into 1/2-inch pieces
4 cups chicken stock
3 cups cooked white rice, warm
1 (15-ounce) can diced tomatoes, drained
1/4 cup chopped scallions, optional garnish

Place the black-eyed peas in a large bowl or pot and cover with water by 2 inches. Let soak for 8 hours or overnight. Drain and set aside.

In a large stockpot or Dutch oven, warm the oil until a few droplets of water sizzle when carefully sprinkled in the pot. Add the onion, green pepper, celery, and garlic, and cook until the vegetables are soft, about 5 minutes. Stir in the oregano, thyme, Creole seasoning, and bay leaves. Season with salt and pepper to taste. Add the bacon and cook, stirring, to brown the bacon, about 4 minutes.

Add the black-eyed peas and chicken stock.

Bring the mixture to a boil over high heat. Reduce the heat to medium-low, cover, and simmer, stirring occasionally, until the peas are tender, about 45 minutes. Add additional water while cooking, if necessary.

Adjust seasonings as needed. Discard the bay leaves. Strain off the remaining cooking liquid and discard.

To serve, mix the black-eyed peas, rice, and tomatoes together in a large bowl. Garnish with chopped scallions if desired.

**SERVES 6 TO 8.**

# JAMBALAYA PASTA

*Jambalaya Pasta is in no way a traditional Louisiana dish, but it does incorporate some of the beloved flavors of that iconic Cajun dish into a tasty pasta meal. My talented friend Jeff Dunham, chef and owner of the Grove Grill in Memphis, occasionally has one of my favorite versions on his menu. Lucky for us, he was willing to share it!*

3 tablespoons olive oil, divided
1/2 cup finely diced yellow onion
  (1 small onion)
1/2 cup finely diced green bell pepper
  (1 small pepper)
2 cloves garlic, minced
1 (14.5-ounce) can diced tomatoes
4 teaspoons tomato paste
1 cup chicken stock, divided
1/4 teaspoon dried oregano
1/4 teaspoon dried thyme leaves
2 teaspoons Worcestershire sauce

Kosher salt and freshly ground black pepper
1/4 cup heavy cream
1 pound large shrimp (16/20 count),
  peeled and deveined, thawed if using
  frozen
1 tablespoon Creole seasoning
  (see page 236 for a homemade recipe)
1/2 pound Andouille smoked sausage,
  sliced into 1/4-inch thick rounds
1 (16-ounce) box farfalle or penne
  pasta, cooked according to package
  directions

In a saucepan over medium-high heat, warm 1 tablespoon of the oil until a few droplets of water sizzle when carefully sprinkled in the pan. Add the onion and green pepper and cook, stirring occasionally, until soft, about 5 minutes. Add the minced garlic and cook until fragrant, about 1 minute more. Add the diced tomatoes, tomato paste, 1/2 cup of the stock, oregano, thyme, and Worcestershire. Stir to combine. Season with salt and pepper to taste. Bring the mixture to a boil over high heat. Reduce the heat to medium-low and simmer

uncovered, stirring occasionally, until the sauce thickens, about 25 minutes. Stir in the heavy cream. Lower the temperature to low and keep warm.

Place the shrimp in a large bowl and toss with the Creole seasoning. In a large saucepan or Dutch oven over medium-high heat, warm the remaining 2 tablespoons oil until a few droplets of water sizzle when carefully sprinkled in the pan. Add the shrimp and cook, stirring occasionally, until the shrimp are lightly browned, 3 to 4 minutes. Transfer the cooked shrimp to a plate and reserve.

Add the sausage to that same pan and cook, stirring, until lightly browned, 3 to 4 minutes. Add the remaining $1/2$ cup chicken stock and cook, stirring up any browned bits on the bottom of the pan with a wooden spoon, for 2 more minutes. Return the shrimp, tomato sauce, and cooked pasta to the pan, and toss to combine. Adjust seasonings as needed. Serve warm.

**SERVES 6.**

**COOKING TIP:** *To adjust the heat, you can add less or more Creole seasoning. A dash of hot sauce would also be a good way to add more spice.*

**V VARIATION:** *Grilled chicken, fish, and even crawfish tails could be added to this dish for a heartier meal.*

# WEEKNIGHT RED BEANS AND RICE

*Red beans and rice is the quintessential Louisiana comfort food. This version is not as creamy as the classic slow-cooked recipe made with dried beans, but it does have all the same flavors with the convenience of being a thirty-minute supper.*

1 tablespoon olive oil
1/2 pound Andouille smoked sausage, thinly sliced into rounds
1/2 cup finely diced yellow onion (1 small onion)
1/2 cup seeded and finely diced green bell pepper (1 small pepper)
1/4 cup finely sliced celery (1 stalk)
1 clove garlic, minced

1/2 teaspoon dried oregano
1/2 teaspoon dried thyme leaves
1 bay leaf
Kosher salt and freshly ground black pepper
2 (15-ounce) cans red kidney beans, rinsed and drained
1 1/2 cups chicken stock
4 cups cooked white rice, warm

In a large stockpot or Dutch oven, warm the oil until a few droplets of water sizzle when carefully sprinkled in the pot. Add the sausage, onion, green pepper, and celery, and cook until the vegetables are soft, about 5 minutes. Add the garlic and cook until fragrant, about 1 more minute. Stir in the oregano, thyme, and bay leaf.

Season with salt and pepper to taste. Add the beans and chicken stock.

Bring the mixture to a boil over high heat. Reduce the heat to medium-low, cover, and simmer, stirring occasionally, until flavors have melded, 20 to 25 minutes.

To serve, discard the bay leaf. Spoon over white rice.

**SERVES 4.**

**COOKING TIP:** *Add your favorite hot sauce for a little heat.*

**DO-AHEAD:** *Cooked red beans store very well in the refrigerator for up to three days.*

**WEEKNIGHT CLASSIC**

# VEGGIES AND SIDES

## EAT YOUR VEGGIES!

I can promise you won't have to say much when you serve the recipes in this chapter. These Southern-inspired recipes transform vegetables into supporting sides that may rival the main course.

While fresh is always best, it is not always an option. When working on these dishes, I was thrilled to learn that I could make showstopper sides using ingredients from my freezer and from cans.

Did you know that frozen vegetables are often healthier and tastier than the fresh varieties? Frozen produce is picked at the peak of ripeness, locking in all the flavor and nutrients when it's at its best. When I can't find locally grown produce, I turn to my freezer.

Unlike most canned vegetables, canned tomatoes offer flavor just as intense as ripe tomatoes. Canned tomatoes are so tasty that in the winter months, I often drain canned diced tomatoes and use them as I would chopped fresh tomatoes. For weeknight meals, canned beans are a convenient and quick alternative to dried beans.

# BARBECUE BAKED BEANS

*I like to use a variety of beans in my Barbecue Baked Beans recipe. This simple twist provides both flavor and color to this classic picnic side.*

½ pound bacon (about 10 slices), cut into ½-inch pieces
½ cup finely diced yellow onion (1 small onion)
½ cup finely diced green bell pepper (1 small pepper)
1 (15-ounce) can black-eyed peas, rinsed and drained
1 (15-ounce) can red kidney beans, rinsed and drained

1 (15-ounce) can pinto beans, rinsed and drained
1 cup barbecue sauce
¼ cup cider vinegar
3 tablespoons prepared mustard
½ cup firmly packed light brown sugar
Kosher salt and freshly ground black pepper

Preheat the oven to 350 degrees.

Place the bacon in a large stockpot or Dutch oven over medium heat and cook, stirring often, until crispy, 3 to 4 minutes. Add the onion and green pepper. Cook, stirring, until the onions and peppers are soft, about 5 minutes.

Add the black-eyed peas, red kidney beans, pinto beans, barbecue sauce, cider vinegar, mustard, and brown sugar. Stir until well combined. Season with salt and pepper to taste.

Bring the mixture to a boil over high heat. Remove from the heat, cover, and place in the oven. Cook until the beans are fork-tender, about 1 hour. Serve warm.

SERVES 6.

**V VARIATION:** *Want a traditional barbecue baked bean dish? Just use three cans of kidney beans instead of the various types listed in this recipe.*

# BROCCOLI CASSEROLE

*This is my friend Gay Landaiche's family's favorite way to eat broccoli. Who wouldn't love this cruciferous vegetable when it's in a cheesy cream sauce with a crunchy topping?!*

2 (10-ounce) packages frozen broccoli
3 tablespoons unsalted butter, divided
2 tablespoons all-purpose flour
1/2 cup 2% or whole milk
1/2 cup chicken stock
1 1/4 cup shredded sharp Cheddar
   cheese, divided

Kosher salt and freshly ground black
   pepper
1/3 cup mayonnaise
1 large egg
1/4 cup finely diced yellow onion
   (1/2 small onion)
1/2 cup panko bread crumbs

Preheat the oven to 350 degrees.

Cook the broccoli according to the package directions. Drain and set aside.

In a medium saucepan over medium-low heat, melt 2 tablespoons of butter. When the butter starts to foam, add the flour and cook, whisking, until thickened, about 1 minute. While continuing to whisk, gradually add the milk and the chicken stock. Increase to medium-high heat and bring the mixture to a boil. Reduce the heat to medium-low and simmer, whisking constantly, until the mixture thickens, 5 to 8 minutes. Remove the pan from the heat. Add 1 cup of cheese and stir until melted. Season with salt and pepper to taste.

In a large bowl combine the cheese sauce, mayonnaise, and egg. Add the broccoli and onions and stir to coat. Place the mixture in an 8 x 8-inch baking dish.

Melt the remaining 1 tablespoon butter in a small bowl. Add the bread crumbs and the remaining 1/4 cup cheese. Stir to combine. Spread the bread crumb mixture evenly over the top of the casserole.

Bake until golden brown, 25 to 30 minutes. Serve warm.

**SERVES 6.**

>> **PANTRY SHORTCUT:** *I like to make my sauces from scratch, but a can of cream of chicken or cream of mushroom soup can be substituted for the base of the homemade cream sauce. Just omit the mixture made with the butter, flour, milk, and chicken stock. Instead heat one can of condensed soup in a small saucepan and add the 1 cup of Cheddar cheese. Stir until melted.*

**V VARIATION:** *Gay tops her broccoli casserole with crumbled Ritz crackers. Since I don't keep those at home because I'd be snacking on them all day, I mix panko bread crumbs and butter to make a similar topping. Either is delicious.*

# CHEESY-JALAPEÑO HUSH PUPPIES

*What would a fish fry be without a good hush puppy? I like to add a little zing to mine by adding jarred jalapeños.*

1/2 cup all-purpose flour
1/2 cup yellow cornmeal
Pinch of salt
1/2 teaspoon baking soda
1/2 teaspoon baking powder
1 teaspoon sugar
1 large egg

1/2 cup buttermilk
1/4 cup minced yellow onion
   (1/2 small onion)
3 tablespoons minced pickled jalapeños
1/4 cup finely shredded sharp Cheddar
   cheese
Vegetable oil, for frying

Place the flour, cornmeal, salt, baking soda, baking powder, and sugar in a large bowl. Stir to combine.

In a small bowl whisk together the egg and buttermilk. Add to the flour mixture and stir to combine. Stir in the onion, jalapeños, and cheese until well combined.

In a large stockpot or Dutch oven, pour enough oil so that there is approximately a 2-inch layer of oil. Over medium-high heat, warm the oil until a few droplets of water sizzle when carefully sprinkled in the pot. In batches so as not to overcrowd the pot, drop the batter by tablespoonfuls into the oil and cook the hush puppies, turning to cook on all sides, until golden brown and cooked through, about 5 minutes. Transfer to a plate lined with paper towels to drain. Serve warm.

SERVES 4 TO 6.

**COOKING TIP:** *I use a small ice-cream scoop that is about the size of a tablespoon to drop my batter into the oil. You could also use two soup spoons. Spraying the scoop or spoons with vegetable cooking spray helps the batter come off more easy.*

# CREAMY STONE-GROUND GRITS

*Stone-ground grits bear little resemblance to the "quick" grits found in most supermarkets. These golden-yellow grits are coarser in texture and offer a richer corn flavor much like Italian polenta. In fact, if you can't find them at your local grocery, polenta is an acceptable substitute.*

**2 cups chicken stock**
**2 cups milk**
**1 cup stone-ground grits**

**Kosher salt and freshly ground black pepper**

In a large saucepan combine the chicken stock and milk. Over medium-high heat, bring the mixture to a boil. Whisk in the grits and season with salt and pepper to taste. Reduce the heat to low, cover, and cook, whisking often, until the liquid is absorbed, 35 to 40 minutes. Adjust seasonings as needed. Serve warm.

**MAKES 4 CUPS.**

**COOKING TIP:** *Boiling grits bubble and are very hot. For this reason it is best to use a saucepan with high sides.*

**VARIATION:** *If you do not have chicken stock, you can substitute water. For an even richer batch of grits, substitute half-and-half or heavy cream for the milk.*

# FRIED GREEN TOMATOES WITH COMEBACK SAUCE

(PHOTO ON PAGE 154)

*There are not many dishes that say "The South" more than fried green tomatoes. I think Southerners use this tangy, tart fruit more than folks from any other part of the country. As for the sauce, this cross between a remoulade sauce and Thousand Island dressing is a Mississippi original. It's so good you'll be "coming back" for more!*

**COMEBACK SAUCE**

1/4 cup grated yellow onion
   (1/2 small onion)
2 cloves garlic, minced
1/2 cup mayonnaise
1/4 cup ketchup
1/4 cup vegetable oil
1 teaspoon Worcestershire sauce
1 teaspoon prepared yellow mustard
1 tablespoon freshly squeezed lemon
   juice
Kosher salt to taste
Hot sauce to taste

**FRIED GREEN TOMATOES**

1/2 cup all-purpose flour
Kosher salt and freshly ground black
   pepper
2 large eggs, lightly beaten
1/2 cup plain bread crumbs
4 medium green tomatoes, sliced 1/4 inch
   thick
Vegetable oil, for frying

■ **TO PREPARE THE COMEBACK SAUCE:** In a medium bowl place the onion, garlic, mayonnaise, ketchup, vegetable oil, Worcestershire, mustard, and lemon juice, and whisk until well combined. Season with salt and hot sauce to taste. Cover and refrigerate until ready to use.

■ **TO PREPARE THE FRIED GREEN TOMATOES:** Place the flour in a shallow bowl and season generously with salt and pepper. Place the beaten eggs in another

shallow bowl. Place the bread crumbs in a third shallow bowl.

■ Generously season the tomato slices with salt and pepper. Working in small batches, lightly dredge both sides of the tomatoes in the seasoned flour, shaking off the excess. Next dip the tomatoes in the egg wash to coat completely, letting the excess drip off. Then dredge the tomatoes through the bread crumbs, evenly coating on all sides. Place the prepared tomatoes on a baking sheet or cutting board.

In a large stockpot or Dutch oven pour enough oil so that there is approximately a 1-inch layer of oil. Over medium-high heat, warm the oil until a few droplets of water sizzle when carefully sprinkled in the pot. In batches so as not to overcrowd the pot, cook the tomatoes until golden brown, about 3 minutes per side. Transfer the tomatoes to a baking sheet lined with paper towels or a baking rack.

To serve, place the fried green tomatoes on a plate. Drizzle with Comeback Sauce.

SERVES 4.

✓ **DO-AHEAD:** *The Comeback Sauce can be made up to two days in advance. Keep covered in your refrigerator until ready to serve.*

# SKILLET-FRIED CORN

*I think this is hands down my family's favorite way to enjoy corn. It is so simple that I am almost embarrassed to call it a recipe. But everyone needs a simple Southern recipe like this one in their repertoire for a super quick side. I use my trusty cast-iron skillet when making it at home.*

4 tablespoons unsalted butter
2 cups corn kernels, thawed if using
   frozen

Kosher salt and freshly ground pepper

In a large skillet over medium heat, melt the butter. Add the corn and cook, stirring often, until warmed through and golden, 5 to 7 minutes. Season with salt and pepper to taste. Serve warm.

SERVES 4.

**COOKING TIP:** *Fresh summer corn cooks up the same way as the frozen. My trick to avoid flying kernels when removing them from the cob is to stand the cob upright in the bottom of a deep bowl as I carefully slice corn off into the bowl.*

# FRIED OKRA POPPERS

*In my house, we like to call these "Okra Poppers." They are just so tasty you can't help popping them into your mouth!*

2 large eggs
¼ cup 2% or whole milk
1 ¼ cups yellow cornmeal
¼ cup all-purpose flour
1 teaspoon cayenne

2 teaspoons kosher salt
½ teaspoon ground black pepper
1 (12-ounce) bag frozen cut okra, thawed
    and rinsed (about 3 cups)
Vegetable oil, for frying

◼ In a medium bowl whisk together the eggs and milk. In another medium bowl place the cornmeal, flour, cayenne, salt, and pepper, and whisk to combine.

◼ Working in small batches, place the okra in the egg mixture and toss to coat. Remove the okra from the egg mixture and shake off the excess. Lightly dredge the okra in the cornmeal mixture, shaking off the excess. Place the prepared okra on a baking sheet or cutting board.

◼ In a large stockpot or Dutch oven, pour enough oil so that there is approximately a 2-inch layer of oil. Over medium-high heat, warm the oil until a few droplets of water sizzle when carefully sprinkled in the pot. In batches so as not to overcrowd the pot, cook the okra, turning to cook on all sides, until golden brown and cooked through, about 5 minutes. Transfer to a plate lined with paper towels to drain. Serve warm.

**SERVES 4.**

🖐 **COOKING TIP:** *When buying cornmeal for fried okra or fried fish, make sure you get plain cornmeal and not a mix that might contain flour and other ingredients.*

Ⓥ **VARIATION:** *If you can find fresh okra in your local market in the summer, definitely feel free to substitute it for the frozen.*

# HONEY-GLAZED CARROTS

*Honey with a zing from freshly squeezed lemon juice makes carrots sing!*

1 (1-pound) bag baby carrots
2 tablespoons unsalted butter
2 tablespoons honey

1 tablespoon freshly squeezed lemon juice
Kosher salt and freshly ground black
   pepper

Place the carrots in a medium saucepan and cover with water. Bring to a boil over high heat and cook until the carrots are fork-tender, 6 to 8 minutes. Drain the carrots and return to the pan. Add the butter, honey, and lemon juice, and cook over medium heat until the mixture is melted and coats the carrots, 3 to 5 minutes. Season with salt and pepper to taste. Serve warm.

**SERVES 4.**

>> **PANTRY SHORTCUT:** *The acid in the lemon juice provides balance to the richness of the honey and butter. If you don't have a lemon in the house, you can substitute white wine vinegar or cider vinegar.*

# PETE'S DIRTY HORSE MASHED POTATOES

*My friend Pete Niedbala first made these potatoes for me over fifteen years ago, and they have remained a favorite ever since. He calls them "dirty" since he leaves the skin on the potatoes, and the "horse" is from the horseradish that makes these potatoes sublime.*

2 pounds small red potatoes, scrubbed and cut into 1-inch pieces
4 ounces (1/2 package) cream cheese, diced
3 tablespoons prepared horseradish

6 tablespoons unsalted butter, divided
1/4 cup half-and-half
Kosher salt and freshly ground black pepper

Preheat the oven to 350 degrees.

In a large stockpot place the potatoes and enough cold water to cover the potatoes by 1 inch. Over high heat, bring to a boil. Reduce the heat to medium-low and simmer until the potatoes are fork-tender, 20 to 25 minutes. Drain the potatoes. While the potatoes are still hot, mash the potatoes through a potato ricer or with a masher. Place the mashed potatoes back into the cooking pot.

Add the cream cheese, horseradish, 4 tablespoons butter, and half-and-half to the mashed potatoes, and stir to combine. Season with salt and pepper to taste. Transfer the potato mixture to a 2 1/2-quart baking dish and top with thin slices of the remaining 2 tablespoons butter. Bake until the mixture is heated through, 15 to 20 minutes. Serve warm.

SERVES 6 TO 8.

**COOKING TIP:** *The heat of the horseradish varies among brands. Three tablespoons gives the potatoes a nice flavor, but let your personal preference dictate how much you use. Pete often puts as many as 5 tablespoons in his! If you're not a fan of horseradish, just omit it for a delicious classic mashed potato dish.*

**PANTRY SHORTCUT:** *Diced frozen potatoes or even store-bought mashed potatoes can be substituted. Just heat according to the package's cooking instructions and mix in the cream cheese, horseradish, and butter as instructed above.*

✔ **DO-AHEAD:** *These potatoes can be prepared and then refrigerated before baking up to one day in advance. Just allow 10 to 15 minutes extra baking time.*

# NICK'S TOMATO GREEN BEANS

*Looking for a new twist on green beans? This is it! This recipe comes from the home kitchen of one of Memphis's top restaurateurs… Nick Vergos of Charlie Vergos's Rendezvous Ribs. Nick uses pantry staples to transform ordinary green beans into a flavor-packed treat.*

2 tablespoons olive oil
1/2 cup finely diced yellow onion (1 small onion)
4 cloves garlic, minced
1 (12-ounce) bag frozen cut green beans, thawed

1/4 cup tomato paste
2 tablespoons balsamic vinegar
1/4 teaspoon dried oregano
1/2 teaspoon dried dill
Crushed red pepper flakes, optional
Kosher salt and freshly ground black pepper

In a large stockpot or Dutch oven over medium-high heat, warm the oil until a few droplets of water sizzle when carefully sprinkled in the pot. Add the onion and cook, stirring frequently, until soft, about 5 minutes. Add the garlic and cook until fragrant, about 1 minute more. Add the green beans and stir to mix. Add the tomato paste, balsamic vinegar, oregano, and dill, and stir until well combined. Add red pepper flakes to taste if desired. Add enough water to just cover, about 2 cups. Season with salt and pepper to taste. Bring to a boil over high heat. Lower the heat and simmer, covered, until the liquid is reduced by half, about 30 minutes. Adjust seasonings as needed. Serve warm.

SERVES 4.

**V** **VARIATION:** *If green beans are in season, you can definitely use fresh to make this recipe. Just be sure to trim them first and add 10 minutes to the cooking time.*

# SKILLET CORNBREAD

*There is really no way around this one—a good Southern cornbread can only be made in a hot cast-iron skillet. My friend Angela English shared with me the secret to having a moist cornbread that still has the ability to crumble beautifully over whatever dish you are serving it with—the additions of mayonnaise and sour cream to a classic cornbread batter. I never would have guessed those two simple ingredients would make a world of difference!*

1 1/2 cups yellow cornmeal
1 teaspoon baking powder
1 teaspoon baking soda
1/2 teaspoon kosher salt
2 tablespoons sugar
1 large egg

1 1/2 cups buttermilk
1/4 cup mayonnaise
1/4 cup sour cream
3 tablespoons unsalted butter, divided
1/3 cup shredded sharp Cheddar cheese

Preheat the oven to 450 degrees. Place a 10-inch cast-iron skillet in the oven to heat.

Place the cornmeal, baking powder, baking soda, salt, and sugar in a large bowl. Whisk to combine.

In a small bowl whisk together the egg and buttermilk. Add the buttermilk mixture, mayonnaise, and sour cream to the cornmeal mixture and stir to combine. Melt 2 tablespoons butter and stir into the batter. Add the cheese and stir to combine.

Remove the hot skillet from the oven and place the remaining 1 tablespoon butter into the hot skillet. Swirl the butter until melted and evenly coating the skillet. Spoon the batter into the skillet. Bake until golden and a toothpick inserted in the center comes out clean, 15 to 20 minutes. Serve warm or at room temperature.

SERVES 8.

**V** **VARIATIONS:** *Folks add lots of different things to their cornbread for extra flavor. A couple of tablespoons of bacon grease can be substituted for some of the butter. Diced jalapeños and pepper Jack cheese can make cornbread have a Tex-Mex flair. A half cup of corn kernels adds both flavor and texture.*

# SMASHED POTATOES

*These have become my family's favorite potatoes. With their crispy exterior and warm, soft interior, these "smashed" potatoes are like the perfect cross between a french fry and a baked potato. My kids love to dip them in ketchup.*

**2 pounds small red potatoes, scrubbed**
**1/3 cup olive oil**
**6 cloves garlic, minced**

**Kosher salt and freshly ground black pepper**

Preheat the oven to 395 degrees. Line two baking sheets with parchment paper.

In a large stockpot place the potatoes and enough cold water to cover the potatoes by 1 inch. Bring to a boil over high heat. Reduce the heat to medium and simmer until the potatoes are fork-tender, 10 to 15 minutes. Drain well.

Place the warm potatoes on the baking sheets. Drizzle half of the olive oil over the top and roll the potatoes around to coat. With the potatoes about 2 inches apart, use the bottom of a glass to carefully flatten each potato until it's about 1/2 inch thick. Sprinkle garlic evenly over the potatoes. Drizzle the remaining olive oil evenly over the top. Season with salt and pepper to taste.

Bake until golden and crispy on the outside, about 25 minutes. Serve warm.

**SERVES 6.**

**COOKING TIP:** *This recipe works best with smaller potatoes. When boiling whole potatoes, the cooking time depends on the size of the potatoes. You'll know they are done when a fork or paring knife is easily inserted into the center of one.*

**V VARIATION:** *Add a tablespoon or two of your favorite dried or fresh herb for added flavor. I like to use rosemary or thyme. Just toss the herbs with the potatoes before baking.*

# SUCCOTASH

*The thing about succotash is that it is both seasonal and pantry friendly. My friend Christy Burch, who shared this recipe, always adds the traditional lima beans and corn in hers, but she loves to mix up the rest of the ingredients depending on the time of year and what she has on hand. In the winter, she adds potatoes or cannellini beans. In the spring, peas and asparagus. And in the summer, diced zucchini, tomatoes, squash, or field peas. Edamame can be used in place of the limas. Basically, the sky is the limit. Use this recipe as a good starting point for your own version.*

1 (14-ounce) can black-eyed peas or
   1 1/4 cups fresh field peas
1 1/4 cup lima beans, thawed if using frozen
1 1/4 cup corn, thawed if using frozen
3 slices bacon
1 cup finely diced yellow onion
   (1 large onion)
1 cup finely diced red, yellow, or orange
   bell pepper (1 large pepper)

1/4 cup thinly sliced celery (1 stalk)
3 cloves garlic, minced
1/2 teaspoon dried thyme leaves
1/2 teaspoon dried rosemary
2 cups chicken stock
3/4 cup half-and-half
3 dashes of hot sauce
Kosher salt and freshly ground black
   pepper

Fill a medium saucepan with water and bring to a boil over high heat. Add the peas, lima beans, and corn, and cook until crisp-tender, about 8 minutes. Drain well and set aside.

In the same saucepan over medium heat, cook the bacon until evenly browned and crispy. Remove with a slotted spoon and transfer to a plate lined with paper towels to drain. Crumble into small pieces once it is cool enough to handle.

Drain all but 1 tablespoon of fat from the pan. Add the onion, pepper, and celery, and cook, stirring frequently, until the vegetables are soft, about 5 minutes. Add the garlic, thyme, and rosemary, and cook until fragrant, about 1 more minute.

Add the vegetables and stock. Over high heat, bring the mixture to a boil. Reduce the heat to medium and simmer until the flavors have melded, 10 to 15 minutes. Stir in the half-and-half, bacon, and hot sauce. Cook until heated through, about 3 minutes. Season with salt and pepper to taste. Serve warm.

**SERVES 6 TO 8.**

COOKING TIP: *Fresh herbs can be substituted for the dried if you have some on hand. Just double the amount used since dried herbs are more concentrated than fresh.*

# SWEET CORN PUDDING

*Studded with corn kernels, the texture of this pudding is like a cross between a custard and soufflé. There are many ways to make corn pudding, but I love the simplicity of this version from the kitchen of my friend Mary Caywood. She says she doubles it when feeding a crowd.*

1/3 cup all-purpose flour
1/4 cup yellow cornmeal
2 tablespoons sugar
2 teaspoons baking powder
1/2 cup (1 stick) unsalted butter, melted
    and cooled to room temperature

1 (14.75-ounce) can creamed corn
1 cup sour cream
2 large eggs
1 1/2 cups corn kernels, thawed if using
    frozen
Kosher salt and freshly ground black pepper

▓ Preheat the oven to 375 degrees.

▓ In a large bowl whisk together the flour, cornmeal, sugar, and baking powder. Add the melted butter, creamed corn, sour cream, and eggs, and stir until well blended. Stir in the corn kernels until evenly combined. Season with salt and pepper to taste.

▓ Spoon the batter into a 2-quart baking dish. Bake uncovered until golden, about 45 minutes. Serve warm.

SERVES 8 TO 10.

» **PANTRY SHORTCUT:** *Substitute 3/4 cup cornbread mix (half of an 8.5-ounce box) for the flour, cornmeal, sugar, and baking powder mixture.*

Ⓥ **VARIATION:** *For a cheesy corn pudding, add 1/2 cup shredded Cheddar cheese to the batter.*

# SWEET ENDINGS

IN MY HUMBLE OPINION, A MEAL IS NOT COMPLETE WITHOUT DESSERT. SO, of course, I had to share some of my favorite "sweet endings" with you.

When you think about it, fresh baked goods are a gift from the heart. Even the simplest baked goods require a little love and attention to prepare.

Baking is a different skill from cooking. Cooking is more casual and forgiving. You can adjust the recipe based on what you have on hand. Baking, however, requires precise measurements. It's almost like a science experiment. Details like sifting flour and having butter softened at room temperature can make a big difference. Once you are in the habit of following recipe instructions exactly, the better your baking will be.

I have shared with you many of my favorites that can be made from simple pantry staples. When baking for the kids or friends, Lemon Squares (page 203), Chocolate Peanut Butter Bars (page 197), and Potato Chip Cookies (page 207) are some of my go-tos. Wrapped up in a box with a little twine, they make a sweet treat that travels well to picnics, school functions, or just to give as a happy.

For dinner parties, pies and cobblers make the perfect ending to a meal. Blackberry Skillet Cobbler (page 192) and Rustic Blueberry-Lemon Tart (page 204) are no-fuss desserts that can be made year-round, thanks to the fruit in my freezer. Bourbon-Chocolate Pecan Pie (page 190) and Apple Crumble Pie (page 186) are pies that my family requests I make on a regular basis.

A little sweet treat puts a smile on everyone's face.

# APPLE CRUMBLE PIE

*This pie combines the best of two classic fruit desserts—a traditional apple pie with the nutty and cinnamon topping of a crumble. At Thanksgiving, I like to add dried cranberries to the apple filling for a holiday treat.*

1 (9-inch) unbaked piecrust, homemade or store-bought
3/4 cup all-purpose flour, divided
1 1/2 cups sugar, divided
2 teaspoons ground cinnamon, divided
1/2 cup chopped pecans
1/2 cup (1 stick) cold unsalted butter, cut into pea-size pieces

6 Granny Smith apples (about 3 pounds), peeled, cored, and cut into 1/4-inch thick slices
2 tablespoons freshly squeezed lemon juice
1/2 teaspoon kosher salt

▪ Preheat the oven to 375 degrees.

▪ Place the piecrust in a deep-dish pie pan and flute the edges if desired. Refrigerate the crust until ready to fill.

▪ In a large bowl stir together 1/2 cup flour, 1/2 cup sugar, 1/2 teaspoon cinnamon, and pecans. Using a fork or pastry cutter, cut in the butter until the mixture looks like pebbles. Refrigerate while preparing the filling.

▪ In a large bowl combine the apples, lemon juice, salt, remaining 1 cup sugar, remaining 1/4 cup flour, and remaining 1 1/2 teaspoons cinnamon. Toss to coat. Fill the center of the piecrust with the apple mixture in an even layer. Crumble the topping evenly over the filling. In case of overflow, place the pie pan on a rimmed baking sheet. Bake the pie until the fruit juices bubble and the topping turns golden brown, 50 to 60 minutes. Remove from the oven and let cool on a rack for 15 minutes before serving. Serve warm or at room temperature.

**SERVES 8.**

🍴 **COOKING TIP:** *Crumbles work well with all types of fruit. Consider using this topping on fillings made from berries, peaches, pears, or cherries. If using frozen fruits, be sure to drain well before adding the other ingredients.*

**✔ DO-AHEAD:** *This crumble topping freezes well. My sister always has frozen fruit and prepared crumble topping in her freezer to quickly whip up dessert for impromptu guests. Store the topping in an airtight container for up to three months. You can also freeze the whole pie, unbaked, for up to one month. Thaw in the refrigerator before baking.*

# BANANA PUDDING PARFAITS

*I just love banana pudding. Something about it always makes me smile. These parfaits are a fun way to serve up this Southern treat.*

2 1/2 cups heavy cream, divided
1/3 cup cornstarch
1/4 teaspoon salt
3 large egg yolks
1/2 cup plus 1 tablespoon sugar, divided

1 teaspoon vanilla extract
2 1/3 cups coarsely crumbled vanilla
   wafer cookies, divided
3 ripe bananas, peeled and sliced
   1/4 inch thick

In a medium saucepan combine 2 cups heavy cream, cornstarch, salt, egg yolks, 1/2 cup sugar, and vanilla. Over medium heat, cook, whisking continuously, until the mixture thickens, about 10 minutes. Remove from the heat and transfer to a large bowl. Transfer to the refrigerator and cool completely, about 1 hour.

In six glasses alternately layer the pudding with 2 cups of the crumbled cookies and the bananas. Cover with plastic wrap and refrigerate until ready to serve.

In the bowl of an electric mixer, whip the remaining 1/2 cup cream and the remaining 1 tablespoon sugar until soft peaks form.

To serve, top the parfaits with whipped cream, the remaining 1/3 cup crumbled cookies, and a banana slice.

**SERVES 8.**

**PANTRY SHORTCUT:** *Instant vanilla pudding can be substituted in a pinch, but the homemade version only takes a few more minutes and tastes much better.*

# BOURBON-CHOCOLATE PECAN PIE

*I took my grandmother's pecan pie recipe up a notch by adding chocolate and bourbon to the mix. For a classic pecan pie, just omit those two ingredients from the recipe below.*

3 large eggs
1 cup firmly packed light brown sugar
1 cup light corn syrup
1 teaspoon vanilla extract
3/4 cup chopped pecans
1 (9-inch) unbaked piecrust, homemade
  or store-bought

1/2 cup semisweet chocolate chips
1 cup pecan halves
2 tablespoons unsalted butter, cut into
  slivers
2 tablespoons bourbon

Preheat the oven to 350 degrees.

Place the eggs in a large bowl and whisk until light but not foamy. Add the brown sugar and stir until there are no lumps. Add the corn syrup and vanilla and stir until well blended. Stir in the chopped pecans.

Evenly cover the bottom of the piecrust with the chocolate chips. Pour the filling over the chocolate chips. Arrange the pecan halves decoratively over the top of the pie. Place tiny slivers of butter evenly over the top of the pie.

Bake until the pie is firm and golden brown, 60 to 70 minutes. As soon as you pull the hot pie out from the oven, evenly sprinkle the bourbon across the top. Let cool to room temperature before serving.

**SERVES 8.**

**COOKING TIP:** *When serving guests, I like to make my pie pretty by decorating the top with pecan halves. When it's just family, I skip that step and just mix the pecan halves in with the filling.*

# BLACKBERRY SKILLET COBBLER

*Cobblers come in many forms: some use biscuits as the topping, others piecrusts, or, as in this recipe, a batter can be used. Whichever way you prefer to make yours, I think bubbly, warm cobblers are the perfect way to enjoy blackberries.*

1/2 cup (1 stick) unsalted butter
1 cup sugar
1 cup all-purpose flour
2 teaspoons baking powder
Pinch of salt

1 cup buttermilk
1 teaspoon vanilla extract
3 cups blackberries, thawed and
   drained if using frozen
Vanilla ice cream, optional

Preheat the oven to 350 degrees. Place the butter in a 10-inch cast-iron skillet (or an 8 x 8-inch baking dish) and place in the oven until the butter is melted but not browned, about 5 minutes.

Meanwhile, place the sugar, flour, baking powder, and salt in a large bowl and whisk to combine. Add the buttermilk and vanilla and whisk until smooth.

Remove the skillet from the oven and pour the melted butter into the batter. Stir to combine. Return the batter to the skillet. Spread the blackberries evenly across the top. Return to the oven and bake until the crust is golden and a toothpick inserted in the center comes out clean, 55 to 60 minutes. Serve warm, with a scoop of vanilla ice cream if desired.

**SERVES 8.**

» **PANTRY SHORTCUT:** *Self-rising flour can be used in this recipe. Use 1 cup self-rising flour in place of the all-purpose flour, baking powder, and salt.*

Ⓥ **VARIATION:** *This same batter could be used with peaches or your favorite berries.*

# NEW ORLEANS BREAD PUDDING WITH WHISKEY SAUCE

*This recipe for New Orleans bread pudding is about as authentic as you can get. My family has been making it for at least three generations, if not longer. My grandmother's trick to a creamy and smooth sauce is to cook the whiskey sauce in a double boiler.*

**BREAD PUDDING**
Unsalted butter, to grease the baking dish
1 loaf French bread (preferably at least a day old), cut in 1-inch cubes (about 8 cups)
3 cups 2% or whole milk
2 large eggs
1 cup sugar
1 tablespoon vanilla extract
1 teaspoon ground cinnamon

Zest of 1 orange
1 cup raisins

**WHISKEY SAUCE**
½ cup (1 stick) unsalted butter, cubed
1 cup sugar
1 large egg
1 cup bourbon whiskey

▪ TO PREPARE THE BREAD PUDDING: Preheat the oven to 350 degrees. Lightly grease a 9 x 13-inch baking dish with butter.
▪ Place the bread in a large bowl. In another large bowl whisk together the milk, eggs, sugar, vanilla, cinnamon, and orange zest. Pour the custard mixture over the bread and toss to coat evenly. Let stand until the bread has soaked up the custard, about 5 minutes. Gently stir the raisins into the mixture.
▪ Pour the mixture into the prepared baking dish. Bake until golden brown and set, 35 to 45 minutes.
▪ TO PREPARE THE WHISKEY SAUCE: In a double boiler, melt the butter. Add the sugar and egg, whisking continuously to prevent the egg from curdling. Cook, whisking constantly, until the mixture thickens, 3 to 5 minutes. Whisk in the bourbon to taste. Remove from the heat and keep warm over the double boiler.
▪ Serve the bread pudding warm with the sauce spooned over the top.

**SERVES 8.**

🍴 COOKING TIP: *Ideally you should use day-old bread for this dish. It is okay to use fresh bread in a pinch. Day-old brioche or croissants can be substituted for the French bread.*

**DO-AHEAD:** *The sauce can be stored in the refrigerator for up to two days. Reheat in a double boiler.*

# CHOCOLATE PEANUT BUTTER BARS

*Oh my! These bars are sinful! My friend Melissa Petersen was right when she told me her recipe was better than any store-bought candy I would find.*

1 1/4 cups (2 1/2 sticks) unsalted butter, divided and softened

2 1/2 sleeves graham crackers

1 cup peanut butter (smooth or chunky), divided

1 cup confectioners' sugar, sifted

1 (12-ounce) bag semisweet chocolate chips

Preheat the oven to 350 degrees.

Melt 3/4 cup (1 1/2 sticks) of butter. In a food processor, finely grind the graham crackers. Remove 3/4 cup of the graham cracker crumbs and set aside. Add the melted butter to the remaining graham cracker crumbs in the food processor and pulse until well incorporated and moist lumps form.

Transfer the graham cracker and butter mixture to a 9 x 11-inch baking dish. Press the crust evenly into the bottom. Bake until set, 8 to 10 minutes. Cool to room temperature on a wire rack.

In the bowl of an electric mixer, beat the remaining 1/2 cup (1 stick) butter, 3/4 cup of peanut butter, and confectioners' sugar until smooth. Stir in 1/2 cup finely ground graham crackers. Spoon the filling evenly over the crust and refrigerate to set, about 5 minutes.

Melt the chocolate in a double boiler. Add the remaining 1/4 cup peanut butter and stir until well combined. Spread the melted chocolate evenly over the peanut butter filling and sprinkle the remaining 1/4 cup finely ground graham crackers evenly over the top. Chill for at least 1 hour. Refrigerate until ready to serve.

**MAKES ABOUT 30 BARS.**

**COOKING TIP:** *To make sure these bars cut nicely, you should slice them with a warm knife. The best way to do this is to dip the knife in warm water and wipe dry in between every cut.*

**V VARIATION:** *You can use either dark or milk chocolate in place of the semisweet if you prefer.*

# PEACHES AND CREAM POPSICLES

*Is there anything more refreshing on a sweltering summer day than an ice-cold popsicle? Homemade fruit pops and creamsicles are a breeze to make. All you need is a blender and some popsicle molds. And if you don't have popsicle molds, don't worry! You can use short paper cups and popsicle sticks. The only hard thing about making these frozen treats is waiting for them to freeze before you can eat them!*

**1 cup peach slices, thawed if using frozen**
**1 cup vanilla yogurt (Greek or regular)**

Puree 1/2 cup of the peaches in a blender or food processor until smooth. Chop the remaining 1/2 cup of the peaches into small pieces.

Place the yogurt, peach puree, and diced peaches in a medium bowl. Stir until well combined. Spoon into the popsicle molds and insert the sticks. Freeze at least 4 hours.

**SERVES 4.**

**COOKING TIP:** *For extra-sweet popsicles, add 1 tablespoon of honey to the mixture.*

**V VARIATION:** *This recipe works well with all summer fruits (fresh or frozen). Try substituting strawberries, blueberries, or raspberries for the peaches.*

# OLD-FASHIONED CARAMEL PIE

*Rich and dense, this pie is definitely a caramel lover's dream. Made-from-scratch caramel pies are far superior to the shortcut ones made with condensed milk caramel. This recipe is from the kitchen of my friend Cindy Ettingoff's grandmother. I guarantee it is worth the effort!*

1 1/2 cups sugar, divided
2 cups 2% or whole milk
3 large egg yolks
4 tablespoons all-purpose flour
1 teaspoon vanilla extract
1 tablespoon unsalted butter

A pinch of kosher salt
1 (9-inch) baked piecrust, homemade or
  store-bought
1 cup heavy cream, chilled
1/4 cup granulated or confectioners' sugar
1 teaspoon vanilla extract

▨ Place 3/4 cup sugar in a medium saucepan. Over medium-low heat, cook the sugar, stirring occasionally, until golden brown and caramelized, about 10 minutes. Keep warm over very low heat.

▨ While the sugar is caramelizing, prepare the custard. In a medium saucepan whisk together the milk and eggs. Add the flour and remaining 3/4 cup sugar and whisk until the mixture is smooth. Over medium heat, cook, whisking continuously, until the mixture thickens, about 10 minutes.

▨ Add the caramelized sugar to the custard, whisking continuously. The caramel may harden, but continue whisking until it has melted and the mixture is smooth and thick, 5 to 8 minutes. Stir in the butter and salt.

▨ Pour the custard into the baked piecrust. Refrigerate until chilled and set, at least 1 hour.

▨ To serve, whip the cream, sugar, and vanilla in the bowl of an electric mixer until soft peaks form. Spoon a generous dollop of whipped cream over each slice.

**SERVES 8.**

🍴 **COOKING TIP:** *It is best to caramelize the sugar and make the custard at the same time so that neither cooks too long. I have to admit the first time I made this pie, I thought I had made a mistake since the caramelized sugar became a hard lump! But just as Cindy had told me, if you keep stirring over medium heat, the caramel melts into the custard.*

**Ⓥ VARIATION:** *Instead of the whipped cream, you can top this pie with a meringue made from the leftover egg whites.*

# LEMON SQUARES

*Lemon squares are a quintessential Southern summer dessert. Tried-and-true, this recipe comes from my friend Emily Smith's grandmother Mimi.*

1 cup (2 sticks) unsalted butter, softened
1/2 cup confectioners' sugar, plus extra
　for dusting the top
2 1/3 cups all-purpose flour, divided

4 large eggs
2 cups sugar
1 teaspoon baking powder
1/3 cup freshly squeezed lemon juice

▨ Preheat the oven to 350 degrees.

▨ In the bowl of an electric mixer fitted with the paddle attachment, beat the butter until creamy. Add the confectioners' sugar and 2 cups flour and mix until well combined. Place the mixture into a 9 x 13-inch baking pan and press evenly across the bottom. Bake until golden brown, about 20 minutes.

▨ In a large bowl whisk together the remaining 1/3 cup flour, eggs, sugar, baking powder, and lemon juice. Pour evenly over the crust. Bake until set, 25 to 30 minutes. Let cool to room temperature on a wire rack. Dust the top with confectioners' sugar.

**MAKES 20 LEMON SQUARES.**

🍴 **COOKING TIP:** *Line your baking pan with parchment paper for easy removal and slicing.*

# RUSTIC BLUEBERRY-LEMON TART

*Here's an easy dessert you can make with this favorite summer berry. Don't fuss over the perfect crust. Instead, whip up a rustic version that is meant to look a little rough around the edges. My family likes it warm with a scoop of vanilla ice cream on the side.*

1 (9-inch) unbaked piecrust, homemade
    or store-bought
2 1/2 cups blueberries, thawed if using
    frozen
Juice and zest of 1/2 lemon
1/2 cup plus 2 tablespoons sugar, divided

2 tablespoons all-purpose flour
1/2 teaspoon ground cinnamon
1/4 teaspoon kosher salt
1 large egg, lightly beaten with
    1 tablespoon water

◼ Preheat the oven to 375 degrees. Line a rimmed baking sheet with parchment paper.
◼ Roll the dough into a 9-inch round about 1/8 inch thick. Transfer to the prepared baking sheet.
◼ In a large bowl combine the blueberries, lemon juice and zest, 1/2 cup sugar, flour, cinnamon, and salt. Toss to coat. Fill the center of the piecrust with the blueberry mixture, leaving a 1 1/2-inch border. Fold the border up and over the blueberries, overlapping every 2 to 3 inches, to make a rim. Brush the rim with the egg wash and evenly sprinkle the remaining 2 tablespoons sugar over the rim.
◼ Bake until the crust is nicely browned and the blueberries are bubbling, about 30 minutes. Remove from the oven and let cool on a rack for 15 minutes before serving. Serve warm.

**SERVES 8.**

Ⓥ **VARIATION:** *Depending on what's in season or what's in your freezer, you can substitute apples, pears, and even peaches for the blueberries.*

# POTATO CHIP COOKIES

*Who doesn't love potato chips? They give these buttery cookies from the kitchen of my talented friend Nancy Kistler a delicious, salty crispness. Bet they become your favorite way to use up all those crumbs at the bottom of the potato chip bag!*

1 cup (2 sticks) unsalted butter, softened
1/2 cup sugar
1 2/3 cups all-purpose flour

1 teaspoon vanilla extract
3/4 cups crushed potato chips (classic style)
1 cup confectioners' sugar

Preheat the oven to 325 degrees. Line two baking sheets with parchment paper.

In the bowl of an electric mixer, beat the butter and sugar until light and fluffy. Add the flour and mix until well blended. Stir in the vanilla and potato chips.

Drop rounded tablespoons of the dough, spaced about 2 inches apart, onto the prepared baking sheets. Bake until lightly browned around the edges, 12 to 15 minutes. Let cool on the baking sheet for 5 minutes. Transfer the cookies to a wire rack to cool completely.

Place the confectioners' sugar in a shallow bowl and roll the cookies in the sugar to lightly coat. Store at room temperature, with waxed paper between the layers, in an airtight container.

**MAKES ABOUT 30 COOKIES.**

**COOKING TIPS:** *Do not refrigerate or freeze the unbaked dough as the potato chips will become soggy.*

*You can also sift the confectioners' sugar over the top of the cookies.*

# MISSISSIPPI MUD BROWNIES

*Since I live on the banks of the mighty, muddy Mississippi River, these sugary-sweet brownies were a must for this book. I think folks up north call them rocky road brownies, but down here in Memphis we refer to them as Mississippi Mud brownies after our chocolaty brown river and the Mississippi Delta pecans that give them crunch.*

**BROWNIES**
1 cup (2 sticks) unsalted butter, plus extra to grease the pan, softened
1/2 cup all-purpose flour, plus extra to flour the pan
4 tablespoons unsweetened cocoa
1/4 teaspoon salt
2 cups sugar
4 large eggs
1 teaspoon vanilla extract

2 cups mini marshmallows
1 cup chopped pecans

**ICING**
1 1/2 cups confectioners' sugar
1/4 cup (1/2 stick) unsalted butter
1/4 cup 2% or whole milk
3 tablespoons unsweetened cocoa
1/2 teaspoon vanilla extract

TO PREPARE THE BROWNIES: Preheat the oven to 350 degrees. Butter and lightly flour a 9 x 13-inch baking pan.

Place the flour, cocoa, and salt into a small bowl. Stir to combine.

In a large bowl cream the sugar and 1 cup butter. Add the eggs, one at a time, and mix until well blended. Stir in the vanilla. Add the flour mixture and stir until just blended.

Pour the batter into the prepared pan. Bake until a toothpick inserted into the center comes out clean, 35 to 40 minutes.

Remove the cake from the oven and sprinkle the marshmallows and pecans evenly over the top. Return to the oven and bake just until the marshmallows start to soften, about 5 minutes. Do not brown the marshmallows. Remove from the oven and set aside while you make the icing.

TO PREPARE THE ICING: Place the confectioners' sugar in the bowl of an electric mixer.

In a medium saucepan over medium heat, cook the butter, milk, cocoa, and vanilla, stirring constantly, until the butter melts, 3 to 4 minutes. Add the chocolate mixture to the confectioners' sugar and beat until smooth.

Drizzle the icing evenly over the warm brownies. Let cool to room temperature, about 1 hour, before cutting into squares.

**MAKES ABOUT 20 SQUARES.**

 **V VARIATION:** *Feel free to substitute your favorite chopped nuts for the pecans.*

# STRAWBERRY CUPCAKES

*With this cute pink icing, these cupcakes make me smile! And what makes me smile even more is that pretty pink color and fruit flavor come naturally from strawberries.*

### CUPCAKES

2 cups sliced strawberries, thawed and
   drained if using frozen
2 cups sugar, divided
1/2 cup water
3 cups all-purpose flour
4 teaspoons baking powder
1 teaspoon salt
1 1/2 cups (3 sticks) unsalted butter, softened
6 large egg whites
2 teaspoons vanilla extract
1 cup buttermilk

### STRAWBERRY CREAM CHEESE ICING

1 (8-ounce) package cream cheese,
   softened
1/2 cup (1 stick) unsalted butter,
   softened
1 teaspoon vanilla extract
5 cups confectioners' sugar, sifted
1 cup diced strawberries, thawed and
   drained if using frozen

■ TO PREPARE THE CUPCAKES: Place the strawberries, 1/2 cup sugar, and water in a medium saucepan. Bring to a boil over medium-high heat. Reduce the heat to medium-low and simmer until the fruit is very soft, about 10 minutes. Transfer the mixture to a blender and puree until smooth. Refrigerate until chilled, about 20 minutes.

■ Preheat the oven to 350 degrees. Line standard muffin tins with paper liners.

■ Place the flour, baking powder, and salt into a medium bowl. Stir to combine.

■ In the bowl of an electric mixer, beat the remaining 1 1/2 cups sugar and the butter until light and fluffy. Add the egg whites, one at a time, and mix until well blended. Stir

in the vanilla and chilled strawberry puree.

■ Reduce the speed to low and alternately in three batches, add the buttermilk and the flour mixture, starting and ending with the milk, and stir until well blended. Fill each liner 3/4 full of batter. Bake until a toothpick inserted into the centers comes out clean, 15 to 20 minutes. Let cool completely on wire racks.

■ TO PREPARE THE ICING: In the bowl of an electric mixer fitted with the paddle attachment, beat the cream cheese, butter, and vanilla until light and fluffy. Add the sugar and beat until smooth. Stir in the strawberries.

■ Generously ice the cupcakes.

**MAKES 24 CUPCAKES.**

**COOKING TIP:** *Depending on the humidity outside and the juiciness of your strawberries, your icing may be a little loose. For a stiffer icing, stir in a little extra confectioners' sugar if needed. I recommend adding ¼ cup at a time until you get the desired consistency.*

**V VARIATION:** *To make this recipe as a whole cake, bake the batter in two 9-inch cake pans for about 25 minutes or until a toothpick inserted in the center comes out clean.*

# RISE AND SHINE

RISE AND SHINE WITH THESE SOUTHERN DISHES THAT ARE PERFECT FOR A lazy weekend breakfast or your next brunch.

They say breakfast is the most important meal of the day. But on busy weekdays, my family is often munching on a breakfast burrito or sipping on a fruit smoothie as we run out the door.

We look forward to Saturday and Sunday mornings when we can leisurely enjoy a filling breakfast. Homemade biscuits are a weekend favorite. We switch between Aunt Lillian's Buttery Biscuits (page 214) and cheesy Pimento Cheese Biscuits (page 226) depending on what else we are serving.

Owen's French Toast (page 225) and Homemade Toaster Tarts (page 228) are dishes that my kids love to get in the kitchen and make with me. I know that one day soon when they get older, I am going to miss this special time cooking with them.

And even though breakfast and brunch are normally served in the morning, I bet your family would enjoy breakfast for supper every now and then! Cheesy Sausage and Egg Casserole (page 218), Candied Bacon (page 217), and Kicked-Up Breakfast Taters (page 222) often find their way to the dinner table in our home.

# AUNT LILLIAN'S BUTTERY BISCUITS

*Do you know those biscuits you get that are soft on the inside but have a buttery, crispy crust on the outside? Well, thanks to my good friend Susan Barcroft and her Aunt Lillian, we can now all enjoy those same tasty biscuits at home!*

2 cups all-purpose flour, plus extra for
   the work surface
1 tablespoon baking powder
1 teaspoon salt

1/4 cup plus 3 tablespoons cold unsalted
   butter, divided
1/2 cup sour cream
1/2 cup regular lemon-lime soda (not diet)

■ Preheat the oven to 450 degrees.

■ In a large bowl whisk together the flour, baking powder, and salt. Cut 3 tablespoons of the cold butter into pea-size pieces. Add to the flour mixture and using a pastry blender or two forks, cut the butter into the flour mixture until the mixture resembles coarse meal.

■ Add the sour cream and soda to the mixture and stir until well combined. It will be a very soft dough.

■ Turn out the dough onto a floured surface and pat into an 8 x 8-inch square. With a sharp floured knife, cut the dough into 9 equal-size squares.

■ Melt the remaining 1/4 cup butter and place in the bottom of a 9 x 9-inch baking pan. Place the biscuits in the pan—they may be touching—and brush the tops with some of the butter from the pan. Bake until golden brown, 15 to 20 minutes.

**MAKES 9 BISCUITS.**

🍴 **COOKING TIP:** *Aunt Lillian makes her biscuits with 7UP. Whichever lemon-lime soda you choose, it is important to use regular (not diet) soda.*

⏩ **PANTRY SHORTCUT:** *Aunt Lillian originally used Bisquick baking mix in her recipe. If you have some on hand, you too can use it as a shortcut. Just use 2 cups in place of the flour, baking powder, salt, and butter mixture in the first step above.*

# CANDIED BACON

*Yes, bacon can be improved upon! This sweet bacon dish is perfect for brunch, or any occasion, for that matter. I have even seen it served as an appetizer at a cocktail party!*

**Nonstick cooking spray**
**¹/₂ cup finely packed light brown sugar**

**12 slices thick-cut bacon**

▨ Preheat the oven to 350 degrees.

▨ Place a wire baking rack onto a rimmed baking sheet. Generously spray the rack and baking sheet with the nonstick cooking spray.

▨ Place the brown sugar in a shallow baking dish. Dredge both sides of each slice of bacon in the brown sugar, making sure the bacon is evenly coated. Place on the wire rack in a single layer with no overlapping pieces.

▨ Bake until the bacon is crispy, 20 to 25 minutes. Serve warm or at room temperature.

**SERVES 4 TO 6.**

🍴 **COOKING TIP:** *I line my baking sheet with foil to help make cleanup easier. The mixture of the bacon fat and sugar can create a sticky mess.*

≫ **PANTRY SHORTCUT:** *White sugar can be substituted for the brown sugar in a pinch. It just creates a stickier, sweeter piece of bacon.*

Ⓥ **VARIATION:** *For a sweet and spicy bacon, add a couple of pinches of cayenne to the brown sugar. My friend Betsy Hood likes to make her candied bacon with peppered bacon for an extra bite.*

# CHEESY SAUSAGE AND EGG CASSEROLE

*I admit it... I am not a morning person. So when I have guests staying over or company coming for brunch, I turn to this casserole that can be assembled the day before. That way, when I am still half asleep, all I have to do is pop it in the oven and a delicious breakfast that will wow my guests will be ready in less than an hour!*

Unsalted butter, to grease the baking dish
1 pound mild breakfast sausage
6 large eggs
4 cups 2% or whole milk

1 cup shredded sharp Cheddar cheese
1 tablespoon chili powder
Kosher salt and freshly ground black pepper
4 slices white bread, cut into quarters

Preheat the oven to 350 degrees. Lightly grease a 9 x 13-inch baking dish with butter.

In a large saucepan over medium-high heat, cook the sausage, breaking up the meat with a wooden spoon until the meat is browned and cooked through, about 8 minutes. Transfer the meat to a colander and drain off the excess fat.

In a large bowl whisk together the eggs and milk until well blended. Stir in the cooked sausage, cheese, and chili powder. Season with salt and pepper to taste.

Place the slices of bread in a single layer in the prepared baking dish. Pour the egg mixture evenly over the bread. Bake until set and golden, 40 to 50 minutes.

**SERVES 8.**

**COOKING TIP:** *Serving a big group? This recipe is easily doubled.*

**DO-AHEAD:** *This casserole can be assembled a day in advance. In fact, I think it's better when made ahead so that the bread has time to soak up the egg mixture. Keep covered in your refrigerator until ready to bake.*

# CHEESY INSTANT GRITS

*When I went to college up north, I always used to get a kick when my "Yankee" friends would ask me what a "grit" was. Grits are basically corn that has been ground and then cooked into a porridge. Believe me, they are so much better than that technical definition sounds! Traditionally a dish served for breakfast, grits are now so popular across the South they have also found their place on the dinner table. When serving them as part of a meal, I like to add cheese to give them a boost of flavor.*

4 cups water
1 cup quick-cooking grits
1 1/2 cups shredded sharp Cheddar
    cheese

1/4 cup 2% or whole milk
1 tablespoon unsalted butter
Kosher salt and freshly ground black
    pepper

In a large saucepan over medium-high heat, bring the water to a boil. Whisk in the grits. Reduce the heat to low, cover, and cook, whisking occasionally, until the liquid is absorbed, about 10 minutes. Stir in the cheese, milk, and butter, and mix until well combined and the cheese has melted. Season with salt and pepper to taste. Serve warm.

SERVES 4 TO 6.

**COOKING TIP:** *Quick-cooking grits have been produced so that they cook in an instant. To prepare stone-ground grits see my recipe on page 162.*

**VARIATION:** *For an even richer batch of grits, substitute half-and-half or heavy cream for the milk.*

# KICKED-UP BREAKFAST TATERS

*Also known as home fries, these seasoned potatoes are the perfect accompaniment to your favorite eggs. The cayenne gives them a delicious kick.*

1 1/2 pounds small red skin potatoes, scrubbed and cut into 1-inch pieces
1/2 cup thinly sliced yellow onion (1 small onion)
2 tablespoons olive oil
1/4 teaspoon cayenne pepper
1/4 teaspoon ground cumin
1/4 teaspoon paprika
1/2 teaspoon garlic salt
1/2 teaspoon kosher salt

▪ Preheat the oven to 400 degrees. Line a rimmed baking sheet with parchment paper.

▪ In a large bowl place the potatoes, onion, olive oil, cayenne pepper, cumin, paprika, garlic salt, and kosher salt. Toss until the potatoes are evenly coated. Place the potato mixture onto the prepared baking sheet in a single layer. Bake, stirring once halfway through cooking, until golden brown and cooked through, about 35 minutes. Serve warm.

SERVES 4.

**⟩⟩ PANTRY SHORTCUT:** *Frozen Southern-style hash browns can be used in this recipe. Just thaw before tossing with the other ingredients.*

# OWEN'S FRENCH TOAST

*This recipe is so easy that even a ten-year-old can make it. In fact, this recipe was taught to me by a ten-year-old! Kudos to my friend Ashley Woodman for teaching her children to cook. Some of my favorite memories from meals are ones where my children helped me prepare them. And remember, Owen says that you know the French toast is ready when it is "crispy as a doughnut" on both sides.*

4 large eggs
1/2 cup 2% or whole milk
4 slices white bread

Nonstick cooking spray
1/2 cup confectioners' sugar

In a large bowl whisk together the eggs and milk until well blended. Place the slices of bread into the egg mixture and turn until both sides are well covered.

Generously spray a nonstick skillet with the cooking spray. Heat the pan over medium heat. Place the bread slices in the pan and cook, turning once, until golden brown on both sides, 6 to 7 minutes per side.

To serve, place the French toast on a plate and sift confectioners' sugar over the top.

**SERVES 2 TO 4.**

*My daughter Sarah makes French toast just like her friend Owen taught her.*

**V VARIATION:** *French toast is also delicious when made with sweet breads, like challah or cinnamon-raisin.*

# PIMENTO CHEESE BISCUITS WITH COUNTRY HAM

*These cheesy biscuit sandwiches marry two of my favorite Southern staples: pimento cheese and country ham. I like to serve them drizzled with honey mustard.*

2 cups all-purpose flour, plus extra for
    the work surface
1 tablespoon baking powder
1 1/2 teaspoons kosher salt
3/4 cup (1 1/2 sticks) cold unsalted butter,
    cut into pea-size pieces

1/2 cup cold buttermilk
2 large eggs, divided
1 1/4 cups grated sharp Cheddar cheese
3 tablespoons finely chopped pimentos,
    drained
1/2 pound country ham, sliced

Preheat the oven to 425 degrees. Line a baking sheet with parchment paper.

In the bowl of an electric mixer fitted with the paddle attachment, combine the flour, baking powder, and salt. With the mixer on low, add the butter and mix until the mixture resembles coarse meal, 30 to 45 seconds.

Combine the buttermilk and 1 egg in a small bowl and beat lightly with a fork. With the mixer on low, add the buttermilk mixture to the flour mixture and mix only until moistened. Add the cheese and pimientos to the dough and mix only until roughly combined.

Transfer the dough to a lightly floured work surface. Knead gently until well combined, 5 or 6 times. Pat out dough to 1/2 inch thick. Using a 3-inch-diameter cookie cutter, cut out biscuits. Gather scraps, pat out to 1/2 inch thick, and cut additional biscuits.

Place biscuits on the prepared baking sheet, about 2 inches apart. In a small bowl lightly beat the remaining egg. Brush the tops of the biscuits with the beaten egg. Bake until golden brown and the biscuits are cooked through, 18 to 22 minutes.

To assemble, cut the ham slices into pieces slightly larger than the biscuits. Using a sharp bread knife, split the biscuits. Fill each biscuit with 1 or 2 pieces of the ham to make a sandwich. Serve warm or at room temperature.

**MAKES 12 BISCUITS.**

 **COOKING TIP:** *Don't feel like cutting out the biscuits? No worries. This recipe also works for drop biscuits. Just scoop 3 to 4 tablespoons of the dough, roll into a ball, lightly press to flatten, and bake as directed.*

# HOMEMADE TOASTER TARTS

*Believe it or not, my kids actually prefer these homemade toaster tarts to the store-bought variety! My family loves strawberry and brown sugar cinnamon the best, so those are the flavors I have shared with you. But you can fill them with just about any flavor jam you like.*

### BROWN SUGAR CINNAMON FILLING
1/3 cup firmly packed light brown sugar
2 teaspoons ground cinnamon, divided
3 teaspoons all-purpose flour

### STRAWBERRY FILLING
3/4 cup strawberry jam or preserves

### TOASTER TARTS
2 (9-inch) unbaked piecrusts,
    homemade or store-bought
1 large egg, lightly beaten with
    1 tablespoon water

### ICING
1 cup confectioners' sugar, sifted
2 tablespoons 2% milk
1/4 teaspoon vanilla extract

▨ Preheat the oven to 400 degrees. Line a rimmed baking sheet with parchment paper.

▨ **TO MAKE THE BROWN SUGAR CINNAMON FILLING**: In a small bowl mix together the brown sugar, 1 teaspoon cinnamon, and flour.

▨ **TO MAKE THE POP TARTS**: Roll out the dough and cut into twelve 3 x 5-inch pieces. Place 6 pieces of dough on the prepared baking sheet. Brush the edges of each rectangle with the egg wash. Spoon about 2 tablespoons of the filling (either the brown sugar mixture or strawberry jam) into the center of each dough rectangle. Top each with the remaining pieces of dough, pressing down to seal on all sides. Press the tines of a fork around all the edges to crimp the dough.

▨ Bake until lightly golden brown, about 20 minutes. Remove from the oven and place the baking sheet on a cooling rack.

▨ **TO MAKE THE ICING**: In a small bowl whisk together the confectioners' sugar, milk, and vanilla. If making brown sugar cinnamon toaster tarts, stir in 1 teaspoon ground cinnamon. If the icing is too thick to spread, add a little more milk to thin. Spoon the icing over the top of the tarts. Serve warm.

MAKES 6 TARTS.

 **COOKING TIP:** *My kids love their toaster tarts garnished with colors. Simply sprinkle colored sprinkles or sanding sugar over the just-iced tarts. You can also add a dash of food coloring to the icing.*

**PANTRY SHORTCUT:** *Frozen puff pastry can be used in place of the piecrust dough.*

**V VARIATION:** *These breakfast treats are pretty sweet. To make 12 toaster tart "minis," cut the dough into 1 1/2 x 3-inch pieces and use just 1 tablespoon of filling in each.*

# HOMEMADE PANTRY STAPLES

NOTHING IS WORSE THAN STARTING A RECIPE AND REALIZING YOU ARE missing a key ingredient!

Homemade versions of common ingredients (some convenience foods and other staples) can easily be whipped up using pantry staples. These simple recipes will help you out when you are in a pinch.

# HOMEMADE CREAM OF CHICKEN CONDENSED SOUP

*I am a big fan of making my own homemade base for recipes that call for canned soups. The homemade version tastes fresher and has none of the additives and extra sodium that accompany canned soups. Throughout the book, I have written my recipes with homemade bases, mentioning that canned condensed soup can be used as a shortcut. Making homemade bases is so simple and takes just minutes. I guarantee it is worth it!*

2 tablespoons unsalted butter
2 tablespoons all-purpose flour
1/2 cup 2% or whole milk

1/2 cup chicken stock
Kosher salt and freshly ground black
  pepper

Melt the butter in a medium saucepan over medium-low heat. When the butter starts to foam, add the flour and cook, whisking, until golden brown, 2 to 3 minutes. While continuing to whisk, gradually add the milk and the chicken stock. Over medium-high heat, bring the mixture to a boil. Reduce the heat to medium-low and simmer, whisking constantly, until the mixture thickens, 5 to 8 minutes. Season with salt and pepper to taste.

**MAKES A LITTLE OVER 1 CUP, THE EQUIVALENT OF 1 (10.75-OUNCE) CAN OF SOUP.**

**(V) VARIATION:** *For cream of mushroom, cook 1 cup finely diced mushrooms in the butter before adding the flour, milk, and stock.*

# IN A PINCH BUTTERMILK

1 cup 2% or whole milk
1 tablespoon lemon juice or white wine vinegar

In a small bowl whisk together the milk and lemon juice or vinegar. Let stand at room temperature until slightly thickened and curdled, 5 to 10 minutes. The mixture will not be as thick as regular buttermilk, but it works just as well in a recipe.

MAKES 1 CUP.

## OTHER BUTTERMILK SUBSTITUTES

3/4 cup plain yogurt thinned with 1/4 cup water

3/4 cup sour cream thinned with 1/4 cup water

# HOMEMADE HALF-AND-HALF

1/2 cup 2% or whole milk
1/2 cup heavy cream

In a small bowl whisk together the milk and heavy cream. Cover and refrigerate until ready to use.

MAKES 1 CUP.

# HOMEMADE BAKING MIX

2 cups all-purpose flour
1 tablespoon baking powder
1 teaspoon kosher salt

3 tablespoons cold unsalted butter, cut
  into pea-size pieces

Place the flour, baking powder, and salt in a medium bowl, and whisk together. Add the butter and using a pastry blender or two forks, cut the butter into the flour mixture until the mixture resembles coarse meal. Store covered in the refrigerator until ready to use.

**MAKES ABOUT 2 CUPS.**

**COOKING TIP:** *This homemade baking mix is a great substitute for store-bought baking mixes, such as Bisquick.*

# HOMEMADE SELF-RISING FLOUR

1 cup all-purpose flour
2 teaspoons baking powder
1/4 teaspoon kosher salt

In a medium bowl whisk together the flour, baking powder, and salt. This mixture will store for several weeks, tightly sealed, in your cabinet.

**MAKES ABOUT 1 CUP.**

# HOMEMADE CORNBREAD MIX

2/3 cup all-purpose flour
1/2 cup yellow cornmeal
3 tablespoons sugar

1 tablespoon baking powder
1/4 teaspoon kosher salt
2 tablespoons vegetable oil

In a medium bowl whisk together the flour, cornmeal, sugar, baking powder, and salt. Whisk in the oil. Use immediately.

**MAKES THE EQUIVALENT OF AN 8.5-OUNCE BOX.**

**COOKING TIP:** *The flour mixture without the oil added to it will store for several weeks, tightly sealed, in your cabinet. When ready to use, whisk the vegetable oil into the dry mix. Use in your recipe just as you would a box of cornbread mix.*

# HOMEMADE BLACKENED SEASONING

4 teaspoons paprika
1 teaspoon dried thyme
1 teaspoon cayenne pepper

1 teaspoon sugar
1 teaspoon kosher salt
1 teaspoon freshly ground black pepper

In a small bowl whisk together the paprika, thyme, cayenne pepper, sugar, salt, and black pepper. This mixture will store for several weeks, tightly sealed, in your spice cabinet.

**MAKES ABOUT 1/4 CUP.**

**COOKING TIP:** *For a little less heat, reduce the amount of cayenne and black pepper.*

# HOMEMADE CREOLE SEASONING

2 tablespoons paprika
2 tablespoons garlic powder
1 tablespoon onion powder
1 tablespoon cayenne pepper
1 tablespoon dried oregano

1 tablespoon dried thyme leaves
2 tablespoons kosher salt
1 tablespoon freshly ground black
   pepper

In a small bowl whisk together the paprika, garlic powder, onion powder, cayenne pepper, oregano, thyme, salt, and black pepper. This mixture will store for several weeks, tightly sealed, in your spice cabinet.

MAKES ABOUT 3/4 CUP.

# WEEKNIGHT CLASSICS

NEED DINNER ON THE TABLE IN A HURRY? HERE IS A HANDY LIST OF DISHES that can be whipped up in about 30 minutes.

1. Corn Salad (page 24)
2. Egg and Olive Salad (page 27)
3. Pantry Quinoa Salad (page 31)
4. Pesto Pasta Salad (page 32)
5. Shrimp Remoulade Salad (page 34)
6. Southern Chicken Salad (page 37)
7. Strawberry Fields Salad (page 38)
8. Three-Bean Salad (page 42)
9. Broccoli and Cheddar Soup (page 48)
10. Creamy Tomato Soup (page 52)
11. Freezer Veggie Soup (page 56)
12. Frogmore Stew (page 59)
13. Lucky Black-Eyed Pea and Collard Green Soup (page 60)
14. Loaded Potato Soup (page 63)
15. Sweet Cornbread and Buttermilk Soup (page 64)
16. Braised Chicken with Mushrooms and Grits (page 70)
17. Grilled Chicken with Peach Barbecue Sauce (page 78)
18. Lemony Chicken (page 83)
19. Honey-Balsamic Flank Steak (page 102)
20. Sausage and Peppers over Cheesy Grits (page 108)
21. Pan-Seared Pork Chops with Drunken Peaches (page 112)
22. Blackened Red Snapper (page 118)

# STOCK YOUR FREEZER

WHEN MAKING THESE RECIPES, MAKE A DOUBLE BATCH TO FREEZE. THIS way you'll always have a home-cooked meal, even if you don't have time to cook.

# MANY THANKS

TO PAUL, FOR YOUR UNWAVERING LOVE AND SUPPORT.

To my sweet Hannah and Sarah, for being the best taste testers, troopers, and daughters a mom could hope for!

To Justin Fox Burks, for making yet another book beautiful with your stunning photography.

To Babcock Gifts, for once again sharing your picture-perfect dishes, linens, and serving pieces. Not only is your collection outstanding; your team is remarkably knowledgeable and delightful.

To Lodge Cast Iron, for sharing the cast-iron skillets and enameled Dutch ovens that enable me to cook delicious Southern dishes just as they should be.

To Gay Landaiche, for using your teacher and proofreading skills to help me be grammatically correct throughout this book.

To the best group of recipe testers an author could ever ask for: Amanda Bowers, Julie Boshwit, Christy Burch, Anne Caraway, Posey Cochrane, Dana Edwards, Cindy Ettingoff, Elizabeth Eggleston, Molly Fleming, Cheryl Followell, Rebecca Fountain, Margaret Fraser, Tom Hanemann, Charlene Honeycutt, Betsy Hood, Paula Hooper, Andrea Hyneman, Lee Anne Kasper, Jan Klein, Tiffany Langston, Beth Lee, Karen McLaughlin, Jeri Moskovitz, Amy Newsom, Jean Owen, Amy Pearce, Karen Perrin, Molly Polatty, Arpana Rawtani, Mary Katherine Redd, Dabney Ring, Mary Alice Ruleman, Lee Schaffler, Macrae Schaffler, Will Sharp, Emily Smith, Darel Snodgrass,

Liz Tindall, Vida Townsend, Anna Tuttle, Jenny Vergos, Michelle Wilson, and Patricia Wilson.

To the talented cooks who shared secrets from their kitchens: Susan Barcroft, Christy Burch, Laura Burns, Mary Caywood, Jeff Dunham, Angela English, Cindy Ettingoff, Rick Farmer, Margaret Fraser, Tom Hanemann, Lucia Heros, Nancy Kistler, Gay Landaiche, Pete Niedbala, Melissa Petersen, Chris Posey, Nevada Presley, Tommy Prest, Lee Schaffler, Leslie Schilling, Will Sharp, Emily Smith, Bob and Betty Sternburgh, Ryan Trimm, Jenny Vergos, Nick Vergos, Bradford Williams, and Owen Woodman.

To my dear friends who lent me their plates, linens, and serving pieces to use in photos: Virginia Sharp, Lee Schaffler, Barbara Hanemann, Justin Fox Burks, Mona Sappenfield, Lou Martin, and Tom and Maritucker Hanemann.

To Kitchens Unlimited for allowing me to photograph in your beautiful showroom. Your selection and design team are unmatched.

To Heather Skelton and all the folks at Thomas Nelson Publishers who helped bring this book to life. I couldn't think of a better team of folks to work with!

To Augusta Campbell, for sharing your stylist talents and helping me pick out just the right outfits and aprons.

To all my Facebook and Twitter friends (I consider you friends, not fans!) who shared ideas and suggestions to make this book the best it could be.

# CREDITS

MANY THANKS TO BABCOCK GIFTS FOR THE USE OF THEIR DISHES, serving pieces, and linens in the following photos:

Pimento Cheese (page 13)

Creamy Spinach Dip (page 17)

Tex-Mex Corn Dip (page 18)

Pesto Pasta Salad (page 33)

Southern Chicken Salad (page 36)

Strawberry Fields Salad (page 39)

Roasted Sweet Potato Salad with Dried Cranberries and Pecans (page 40)

Broccoli and Cheddar Soup (page 49)

Creamy Tomato Soup (page 53)

Freezer Veggie Soup (page 57)

White Bean and Country Ham Soup (page 66)

Braised Chicken with Mushrooms and Grits (page 71)

Chicken Divan (page 73)

Chicken Fricassee (page 74)

Chicken Pot Pie with Buttermilk-Herb Biscuits (page 68)

King Ranch Chicken (page 81)

Lemony Chicken (page 82)

Pa's Herbed Chicken Parts (page 85)

Peanut-y Fried Chicken Strips with Maple-Dijon Dipping Sauce (page 87)

Mimi and Pop's Marinated Grilled Chicken (page 89)

Slow Cooker Cola Chicken (page 90)

Fried Pork Medallions with White Milk Gravy (page 97)

Grillades (page 101)

Louisiana Meat Pies (page 92)

Sausage and Peppers over Cheesy Grits (page 109)

Pantry Pork Tenderloin (page 110)

MANY THANKS TO LODGE CAST IRON FOR THE USE OF THEIR PIECES IN
the following photos:

# INDEX

freezer
pantry essentials in, xxiv–xxv
storing flour and cornmeal, xx
Freezer Veggie Soup, 56
french toast, Owen's French Toast, 225
fricassee, 75
Fried Green Tomatoes with Comeback Sauce,
164–165
Fried Okra Poppers, 168
Fried Pork Medallions with White Milk
Gravy, 96–97
Frogmore Stew, 59
frozen vegetables, 155
fruit
frozen, xxiv
popsicles, 198
tarts, 204

## G

garbanzo beans, Three-Bean Salad, 42
Good Old Potato Salad, 28
graham crackers, Chocolate Peanut Butter
Bars, 197
grains, essentials, xviii
Grandma's Meatloaf, 98–99
grapes, Southern Chicken Salad, 37
green beans, Nick's Tomato Green Beans,
175
Grillades, 100
Grilled Chicken with Peach Barbecue Sauce,
78–79
grits
Cheesy Instant Grits, 221
Creamy Stone-Ground Grits, 162
Grillades, 100
Sausage and Peppers over Cheesy Grits,
108
Tamale Pie, 114–115

## H

half-and-half
Creamy Spinach Dip, 16
Homemade Half-and Half, 233
Pete's Dirty Horse Mashed Potatoes, 172

Succotash, 180
ham
Pimento Cheese Biscuits with Country
Ham, 226
White Bean and Country Ham Soup, 64
herbs, xxvii
Homemade Basil Pesto, 32
homemade staples
Homemade Baking Mix, 234
Homemade Blackened Seasoning, 235
Homemade Cornbread Mix, 235
Homemade Cream of Chicken Condensed
Soup, 232
Homemade Creole Seasoning, 236
Homemade Half-and Half, 233
Homemade Self-Rising Flour, 234
In a Pinch Buttermilk, 233
Homemade Toaster Tarts, 228
Honey-Balsamic Flank Steak, 102–103
Honey-Glazed Carrots, 171
Hoppin' John, 149
Horseradish Encrusted Grouper with Lemon
Butter Sauce, 122–123
Hot Onion Soufflé Dip, 7
hush puppies, Cheesy-Jalapeño Hush Puppies,
161

## I

icing, 208
for Homemade Toaster Tarts, 228
Strawberry Cream Cheese Icing, 210
Indoor Smoky Pork Butt, 104–105

## J

jambalaya
Andouille Jambalaya, 140–141
Jambalaya Pasta, 150–151
Jelly Jar Salad Dressing, 45

## K

Kalamata olives, Pantry Quinoa Salad, 31
kale, Lucky Black-Eyed Pea and Collard Green
Soup, 60
ketchup